The Unbeatable Dream

Margaret, Jack and Dorothy Millar, 1985

The Unbeatable Dream

THE FIRST 25 YEARS OF NAPILI KAI BEACH CLUB

by
Jack, Margaret
and Dorothy Millar
as told to and written
by Brooke Brown

Edited and Produced by
Richard P. Wirtz
Studio Maui
55B N. Church St., Wailuku, HI 96793

Printed in the United States by
Skipper Printing and Graphics, Inc.
Wailuku, HI and
Arcata Graphics Fairfield
Fairfield, PA

DEDICATION

To the original eleven shareholders:
Cece and Barbara Atkinson
Herb and Donne Bliss
Orbie and Edith Boake
Del and Dorothy de La Mothe
Jack and Grace Gregory
Eileen Grove (now Nicholson)
Ross and Eleanor Leydon
Jack and Margaret Millar
Slim and Helen Wheeler
El and Pearl Williams
Lloyd and Helen Williams
and
to all the other brave souls who over the years have
risked their investment monies to build the dream
and
to all future believers in the dream who will risk
their monies to see it all bear fruit.

TABLE OF CONTENTS

TABLE OF CONTENTS

CHAPTER ONE

Love At First Sight

Mud, mud, glorious mud,
  Nothing quite like it for cooling the blood;
Follow me follow, down to the hollow.
  There we will wallow in glorious mud!

Whoever would have guessed how the words of that ditty would ring in the ears of Jack, Margaret, and Dorothy Millar? Certainly, not they! Nor did they imagine the challenges posed by tidal wave warnings, floods, and fire which were to confront them when they pursued a dream.

The dream was the offspring of a great love affair—a love affair which began in 1957 and was to continue into the present. The principals were three Canadians and the island of Maui, second largest in the Hawaiian chain.

Jack Millar, an honorably discharged wing commander from the Royal Canadian Air Force, and his wife, Margaret, sought respite from the cold Vancouver winters in Waikiki. Like many visitors, they fell passionately in love with Hawaii and established a pattern of yearly visits.

Before long, however, the increasing growth and congestion became a source of unhappiness. Jackhammers and traffic noises drowned out the sounds of the birds, and the trade winds carried construction dust and exhaust fumes. So, when Jack was told of a nice piece of available property situated on a small bay on Maui, he and Marg arranged to fly there immediately.

Upon arrival, they rented a U-drive car and found their way to Napili Bay, where they were directed to the exact piece of property that was available. The half-acre parcel fronted the bay, which was then shrouded by giant kiawe (algaroba) trees. The dense, thorny-branched trees which grew to the beach and the preponderance of skunk cabbage made it impossible to walk into the property without difficulty. But the peace, the sun, the sea breeze, and the gentle lapping of the ocean won Jack and Marg's hearts: they were enamoured with this spot. And so, the seeds of a dream were planted to go along with the budding love affair.

Jack returned to Vancouver, determined to acquire the parcel. Inquiries led him to Herb Bliss, who was the leasing manager for a large Cadillac dealer in Vancouver. Bliss had also visited the Napili site and was interested in its acquisition. Since the owner was unwilling to sell the property at any price, the two men discussed the possibility of taking out a lease and putting a small building on the property. They could create a little Shangri-la!

Jack was then the president of Columbia Metal Rolling Mills and spent most of his days in airplanes flying between the three high-speed steel and aluminum-fabricating plants in Toronto, Winnipeg, and Vancouver and the sales offices around Canada. He gave little thought to living in Hawaii but the idea of developing a little resort with some friends had great appeal.

After Herb wrote a letter to several friends whom he thought might be interested, he and Jack met with them and put forth the resort idea. The suggestion was that anyone interested in joining them put up $500. Several individuals stepped forward: thus, the effort to form a corporation was underway.

Jack would be the president of the corporation, Herb Bliss, the vice president, and Del de La Mothe, the secretary, and Dorothy, the treasurer. These three men called another meeting and asked this time for a $5,000 minimum investment. Ten people promised $10,000 apiece. In 1960, they incorporated in Hawaii under Hawaiian law as Napili Kai, Ltd., a Hawaii corporation. A resort was born!

A 30-year lease was agreed upon, an architect was hired to design a modest 16-room resort, and the project was put out to bid to local builders on Maui. But, because Napili was a remote area at the end of the coastal road, Maui builders were not interested in the job.

Lahaina Wing almost completed. Opened March 1962.

The original building at the Napili Kai Beach Club was the Lahaina Wing and was not built without a struggle. Once the corporation had the lease, the directors approached Maui banks for loan assistance for the building's construction since the corporation's funds were only slightly in excess of $100,000. The banks were not interested.

Another meeting was held and shareholders were asked for an additional $10,000 or to find a willing friend. The directors changed the value of their stock from $1 to $2. The outcome was that the corporation expanded to 25 members and had enough capital to pay for the building of the Lahaina Wing in cash, and hired David Anderson, a young Honolulu contractor. In his own plane, David flew his Honolulu crew to Maui where the men would work a 10-day stint before going back to Oahu for a three-day break.

At that point in time, 1961, the only other resorts on Maui were the Hana Resort and the Maui Palms which was operated by Lyle Guslander. The Pioneer Inn had 8–10 rooms, and George Tam's Banyan Inn was the only other eating house. Plans for a golf course at Kaanapali were underway, but Napili was still a remote area with no drawing card.

Jack made many trips to Maui from Vancouver during the construction period to oversee the work. His wife and daughter Elizabeth, now Elizabeth Warren a Vancouver nurse, travelled with him. In August, 1961, Jack was so smitten with Napili that he wrote the following to his Canadian friends:

The Bay in summer is even more beautiful than in winter. The climate drier than that experienced in Honolulu and much more pleasant. Sleeping each night was a thrill because of the constant breeze and relatively dry air which mixed with the boom of the surf slapping the beach was a delightful experience. In my life, I have never before slept under such delightful circumstances. Water in the Bay was strikingly clear. Whilst snorkeling, I could see at least 50 feet in a forward direction. I believe our location is as beautiful as anything in all the Islands. Once people hear of it, we will have a very high occupancy rate.

When the resort's doors opened on March 26, 1962, a single room cost $10, a double $15, and a suite could be had for

$20. But, business was so slow that by June the rates were cut in half in an attempt to attract tourists, and that bargain rate was offered until the next fall! While Millar, Bliss, and de La Mothe decided the policy for the Napili Kai Beach Club, management of the resort was given to Dorothy Sudbury (now Millar). Dorothy, who had been born to British parents and raised in Shanghai, left China in 1949 and went to Vancouver where she worked as Jack's executive secretary, steel buyer, and an officer of the corporation. She flew back and forth regularly to do the books, engage managers, hire maids, and, in general, supervise the operation. Later, when Jack and Marg's children had grown and left home, Jack and Margaret adopted Dorothy since she had become such an invaluable member of their family and affairs.

The enthusiasm for Maui was contagious enough to warrant planning a second building, the 32-room Honolua Wing, and a small restaurant, The Teahouse of the Maui Moon. Funding the expansion was a nightmare, but enough shares were purchased at $4 apiece by original Canadian shareholders, and other return guests to initiate the project which was completed in December of 1963.

The Columbia Rolling Metals Company was sold in 1962, and Jack thought of buying another Vancouver business. However, his fellow Napili Kai directors pursuaded him to move to Napili for a year to find out why Napili Kai, Ltd., was sustaining annual losses. Jack and Marg sold their Vancouver home and made the move in 1963, bringing Dorothy with them. Little did the Millars know what they were starting when they left Canada and moved to Maui for "one year!" Later, Jack was to laughingly remark,

"We never intended to stay...but we ended up getting caught!"

The trap promised Shangri-la while concealing a wonderfully crazy carnival that would demand ever increasing time on the part of the Millars.

Meanwhile, Jack had arranged with Ruth McMann (now Nettleship), a former Vancouver travel agent who lived on Oahu, to meet them when their P & O liner, the *Oriana*, docked in Honolulu. Jack, hoping to soften the moving blow to Marg and Dot, had asked Ruth to surprise the women with a pair of poodle puppies. His ploy worked, and Marg and Dot were delighted with the household additions, Steel and Pom Pom.

A twin-engine Beechcraft transported the Millars and their effects, save their Fiat 500 which was consigned to a barge, to Maui. Amazingly, P & O had accepted the little car as excess baggage and charged them only $30! Joe Amaral— the charming and irrascible bellhop, part-time taxi driver, and groundskeeper— met the Millars when they deplaned in Kaanapali.

CHAPTER TWO

Building The Dream

Napili Kai, Ltd., had leased a two-acre land parcel behind the existing buildings, and the Millars decided to move the old World War II quonset hut which had been on the property to the far corner. Moving day arrived, and the mover assured the trio that crossing the swale which ran from the road to the ocean would not pose a problem. The mover put the quonset on his flatbed and drove away. Within minutes, a man was high up a large kiawe tree sawing off branches which were overhanging the swale so that they wouldn't interfere with the passage of the quonset's roof. Then, as the flatbed proceeded into the slight ditch, the Millars heard a terrible crunch. The quonset had broken in half! It was small consolation that it had not completely broken apart.

Finally, the men backed the flatbed into Jack's meticulously-selected site, which he had marked with pins. Since Jack and Marg had had to leave the property earlier that afternoon, Dot Millar was in charge of the operation; and, she insisted that the men place the quonset on Jack's pins. Ten or 15 tries later, one of the men said,

"Hey, lady, dees da bes we can do!"

At that point, Dot decided that if Jack were not satisfied with the quonset being 12 inches from his pins, he would have to move it! Needless to say, the cottage has remained on that spot to this very day.

The Millars loved living in the cottage. Unfortunately, because they lived on the property they were called when anything went wrong—broken toilets, sickness, lost keys, heart attacks—in the middle of the night. But, such disadvantages were far outweighed by being able to take an early morning dip in the blue Pacific or to sit on the beach in the evening and drink a toast to a flaming sunset.

The women always answered the door because Jack, a sound sleeper, never heard the knocks. Someone once asked Jack how he slept so soundly, and he laughingly replied,

"Why shouldn't I? I have two watchdogs!"

The Napili Kai Beach Club was formally opened by Eddie Tam, who arranged for the dedication of the resort on December 14, 1963. "Mayor" Tam, as he was known, was a Chinese immigrant and colorful local politician. Officially, he was chairman of the county board of supervisors, which directed affairs on Maui. The flamboyant mayor was proud to be the encourager of Napili Kai's development, showing Mauians the direction of the future.

The blessing, a lovely blend of Christianity and the lore of Hawaiiana, was done by Reverend John Kukahiko, a kahuna and preacher and was truly moving. Maile leis, a perogative of royalty in earlier days, were in abundance, and the dedication was a festive occasion. At this ceremony, attended by some 350 people, "Mayor" Eddie Tam presented Jack Millar with a Key to Maui.

Tam returned often to Napili Kai Beach Club. He would drive onto the property in his big Cadillac, sounding his horn. Then, his voice would blast over his police loudspeaker saying,

"Jack Millar, where are you? This is your mayor! Present yourself! Where are you?"

All of the guests would hear him, and the occasions were lots of fun.

The Millars new life at Napili Kai was far from dull. Within their first year at the resort, there were several tidal wave warnings. The Millars were startled by their first warning shortly after their arrival. The police called at midnight to say that everyone must evacuate since the wave

Opening of Honolua Wing and dedication of it and the Lahaina Wing, December 1, 1963. From left to right: Dorothy Sudbury (now Millar the present general manager), Mrs. Helen Berwick (shareholder), Jack Millar (president and managing director), Rev. John Kukahiko, Mayor Eddie Tam, Mrs. Margaret Millar, Ruth McMann (now Nettleship), and Jack's son Dewar Millar (now director).

was travelling at 500 mph and was due in one and a half hours.

The Millars raced through the resort, knocking on all doors and ordering guests to come to the cabana for coffee and instructions immediately. People were told to place their luggage on the dresser or bed, take a pillow, a blanket, and their valuables, and move to higher ground—Pineapple Hill!

Once the Millars had attended to the guests, they began to plan their own evacuation. It fell to Margaret to pack the car.

Through all of this, the civil defense siren wailed continuously as the guests and staff scrambled helter-skelter.

Much later, when the all-clear was issued and people stumbled back to their rooms, the Millars were astounded to discover what Margaret had packed: running shoes, dog food and leashes, one banana, toothbrushes, deodorant, a bottle of Coke, and a bottle of scotch!

When Jack asked Dottie what she had done with her treasured fur stole, she replied,

"I thought I'd look pretty funny in shorts, thongs, and fur so I took a chance!"

Happily, the wave-tracking system improved after several more warnings, and Napili Kai today has not had a warning in years. Nor, has Napili suffered wave damage — from the direction of the ocean!

In a small resort, such emergencies underscore the personal contact between staff and guests. The Millars sensed that their guests felt closer to the staff than a person would in a larger chain hotel, and this observation was upheld in an incident at the front desk. In the early days, the staff consisted of five people: Jack, Marg, Dorothy, Betty the bookkeeper, and Ruth, who had left her job as a travel agent in Honolulu to join the Millars on Maui and oversee the front desk and reservations.

One day, a nosy guest who seemed always to be hanging around the front desk happened to see Marg in the office. Marg only worked in the office when extra help was needed for sticking stamps or other occasional jobs. The man pointed his finger at Ruth, then Betty, and then Dottie. Finally, he addressed Ruth,

"I know what you do, and I know what she does; and, I know what she does. But, I don't know what she does," pointing to Marg.

Ruth responded immediately.

"Oh, she has the best job of all: she sleeps with the boss!"

The look on the man's face amused the staff for days to come, and they were amused that he didn't spend anymore

View of the bay from the Honolua Wing, 1980s.

time hanging around the front desk.

Stocking a Maui resort was a challenge in the early 1960s. Danny, the chef, had to wait three months for shipment of a cleaver which, had been ordered in Wailuku. Furthermore, the stores seemed incredible to Marg as they sold some of everything. At one point, Marg purchased paint brushes from Imura Jewelry, which also stocked paint and turpentine.

All of the shopping for the rooms had to be done in Honolulu, which then had only a few warehouses. Months were required for delivery of items. Once, 20 identical pillows were needed, and Sears Roebuck could only supply six of them. Furthermore, Sears Roebuck needed a six-month delivery time to fill the rest of the order.

The Millars made the rounds of the main stores in Honolulu when they needed dishes for the Teahouse Restaurant and could only find one complete set which was a service for 12...and Napili Kai required dozens of sets! For many years, Napili Kai's china came from Japan. Doing business in a rural spot on a remote island just wasn't like downtown Vancouver.

CHAPTER THREE

Onward And Upward

Napili Kai's first year was a financial disaster since income hadn't covered the wages or taxes. Maui was not a well-known tourist destination at that time, and the Napili Kai Beach Club was too small to make much of an impression on the travel market.

Things changed, however, with the opening of the Royal Lahaina Resort at Christmas, 1962. The Sheraton at Black Rock opened in January, 1963, and the golf course went into operation. Maui was thrust into the news, especially with Sheraton's worldwide promotion. The sleepy town of Lahaina awoke and started to bustle with activity. And, the world of visitors discovered the quiet little bay out at Napili.

Tourists jumped on the bandwagon, and more and more vacationers rode it to Napili Kai. Of course, as the number of guests increased, so did the innkeepers' problems! Living on the resort property meant that the Millars were available 24 hours a day to take care of any such problems. Many of these problems occurred at night. One evening, Jack accompanied Doug Tihada on his 11 p.m. rounds of the property, making sure everything was as it should be. The noise of crashing dishes coming from the second floor of the Lahaina Wing caught their attention, and the two men rushed to the room and pounded on the door. Giggling—and another smash!—was the only response! Jack opened the door with his master key, and he and Doug burst into the room.

A tiny old woman, highly intoxicated, was furious at her husband, who was hiding in the bathroom from her. He, also drunk, would open the bathroom door sporadically and giggle and tease her. She, then, would hurl another dish at him; but, he would block her pass with the door. Jack rushed to the woman, clad only in her nightgown, and commanded her to stop and sober up! Furthermore, he told her that she and her husband must leave the hotel in the morning.

The next morning, the sober elderly couple apologized to Jack, offered to pay for the wreckage, and pleaded to stay at Napili Kai. Jack felt that money alone could not replace everything in a little place on Maui at that time because it might take three months to replace the dishes so he lectured them. He allowed them to stay, and there were no more problems with them. Fortunately, that couple's act has never been repeated.

A typical Mai Tai Party.

One evening, about 9 p.m., the three Millars were dining at the Teahouse of the Maui Moon when someone ran in and reported that there was a man having a problem down at the beach. The Millars and Douglas Tihada, the manager of the Teahouse restaurant, dashed to the beach. They discovered that a guest of the Beach Club, who had only moments earlier left the Teahouse with his wife for an after-dinner stroll, had suffered a heart attack. Douglas endeavoured to perform C.P.R. on the man—who was already dead on the Millars' arrival.

The body was placed on a surfboard which was used by the Beach Club for rescue purposes. But, the question then was: what would the Millars do with the body? Marg Millar took the widow to her room to console her while Jack, Dot, and Doug telephoned the police to advise them of the incident. The police instructed them to summon a doctor, who would certify the man's death.

While Dot was talking to the police, the body of the gentleman was placed in some bushes so it would not alarm the other guests. When the doctor arrived and certified that the gentleman had indeed died of a heart attack, the Millars were informed that Napili's side of the island was without a mortuary. Furthermore, they were told that all mortuaries on Maui were closed at that hour. Panic! The Millars couldn't leave a body in the bushes all night! After many telephone calls and a couple of hours of argument, an ambulance finally arrived to take away the body.

A humorous part of this whole incident occurred when Dot telephoned the police to report the death and identified herself to the policeman. He responded promptly saying,

"Young lady, you drive too fast!"

Completely taken aback and wondering what that had to do with a dead body in the bushes, she asked him what he meant. Apparently, earlier that day Dot had passed a car on the road, only to discover that there were two more cars in front of the car she meant to pass. Because she was already committed, she passed all three—only, the front car was a police cruiser! The officer didn't stop her or give her a ticket, but he must have taken down her license number! That's how small Maui was in those days!

Napili's lovely white sand beach has been the site for many hair-raising situations. Occasionally, the calm bay gives rise to a swell, and waves pound the beach. A sign is posted, warning guests to stay out of the dangerous water.

One such day, Jack looked out across the beach and saw a man frantically waving his arms and yelling for help. This man had first come to Jack's attention when the man made it known that he was a great friend of another large Maui resort's developer and financier. Furthermore, this pompous individual wanted it known that he was a very important man in the Los Angeles area.

Apparently, this man had walked through the lobby earlier that morning in his bathing suit and had been questioned by Paddy Jacobsen, who was working at the front desk.

"You're not going in that water, are you?" she had asked.

"Young lady, I'll decide when my sons and I will go into the water. My sons are great swimmers," he replied sharply.

He then proceeded to boast of his sons' swimming prowess, telling her what university teams they had been on.

Paddy was quite upset and worried, but there was nothing she could say since the man refused to listen to her.

The man and his sons had gone to the beach, and the youths had dived through the first waves. Soon they found that ocean swimming was different from being in a pool, and they were unable to get back to shore. The old man panicked.

His sons were fished out by a long rope. When a wave receded, someone on the beach would run as close as possible toward the water and hurl the rope to them. The rescue attempt took 15 minutes and left everyone, particularly Jack, shaken.

The following day, the father found Jack in his small

office in the Lahaina Wing and asked to speak privately to him. Jack escorted him to the swimming pool area and was shocked by what the man had to say.

The fellow wanted to make sure that Jack knew how influential he was and to tell Jack that if anything had happened to his sons the previous day, the man would have owned Napili Kai—not Jack!

Needless to say, these words were not received lightly by Jack Millar.

"If I own this hotel as you suggest, then I am the boss. Suppose you get your wife and belongings and be out of this hotel within two hours or I'll have the police come and throw you off the property!" thundered Jack.

The man was absolutely indignant...but, he packed his things and left.

In addition to human troubles, Napili Kai had to contend with wildlife. A number of cows, pigs, stray dogs, and cats roamed the property and damaged the putting green. The dogs and cats bred at a rapid rate and became horrid pests. Soon, workers made almost-daily trips to the pound, which was in Kahului. Rats built large nests in the kiawe trees, and

The "Puka-puka" rock, a historical landmark.

Original Tea House of the Maui Moon.

the Millars constantly struggled to reduce the rodent population.

There were many such problems that arose in the early days. Being at the end of the road, Napili Kai depended on cesspools for their sewage, and the cesspools posed more problems than anything else. Management had to find a way to take care of all problems since there was no government support mechanism developed yet on Maui. Napili Kai's maintainance man was Robert Hirata. Because Hirata possessed an extremely poor sense of smell, plumbing problems were assigned to him. Sometimes, he needed an assistant; and, his helper was frequently Dorothy.

Once, the plumbing was backed up into four rooms, and Robert called upon Dorothy to assist him. Robert removed the iron plate from atop the cesspool, ordered Dorothy to duck her head down into the hole, and instructed Margaret to hold onto Dorothy's feet. Robert's task was to run a long snake

Another view of the original Tea House.

through the rooms' toilets while poor Dorothy, flashlight in one hand and pinching her nostrils with her other hand, peered into the cesspool to see if anything new appeared. Robert's voice was heard in the distance, calling,

"Do you see anything?"

One can imagine Dorothy's delight when a dozen or so swimming suit bags came through the muck— a child's idea of fun?"

Another time, Dorothy phoned the county of Maui, which owned the only pump wagon on Maui, for assistance. They pumped the largest cesspool and informed Dorothy that the grease from the restaurant's kitchen and the rooms' kitchenettes coated the cesspools' inner walls like a skin and prevented absortion of the sewage into the earth.

Dot's response was

"Show me!"

So, once again, Dorothy's head disappeared into a cesspool opening, and she observed the glistening greasy skin they described. Chemicals did not work. The solution was to explode a small charge of dynamite inside the cesspool; then, the system would work for a few more months.

On another occasion, Dorothy phoned the county of Maui and asked them to pump one of the large cesspools next to the Teahouse Restaurant. A crew arrived promptly, assessed the situation, and told the Millars that two or three loads would be necessary to empty the cesspool.

When the tank was full with the first load, the fellow in charge told Jack that he would not be gone long. Jack figured the man would have to drive at least as far as Lahaina to empty the tank and was surprised when the empty wagon returned for its second load within 10 to 15 minutes. Later that afternoon when the Millars returned to their cottage, Margaret asked,

"What is that terrible smell around here?"

The Millars went outside to find the cause of the stench and were shocked to see an oozing mass creeping down the hillside between the bushes in the direction of the drainage ditch. The overpowering stink lasted for many days thereafter—until the ground dried out. When questioned later, the driver admitted that he had unloaded the truck just around the corner from the resort on the property which today supports the tennis court, shop, and maintenance area.

The Millars had to truck in loads of soil and lime with which to cover the sewage and spread the loads—no easy task! Eventually, the resort built a sewage treatment facility that hooked all the cesspools into one digestive plant, and this became the method by which sewage was handled.

That first year passed quickly for the Millar trio, and the thought of moving back to Vancouver receded. Initially, living in such a remote area of Maui, they were bothered by the lack of people to talk to. The Millars' sophisticated social life had changed dramatically since their Vancouver days. But, they adjusted and developed a social life around their guests, who were exciting people.

Beach cabana with each guest having their own booze locker.

An enjoyable social event had evolved at the hotel. A liquor locker with its own key was reserved in the cabana for each room. Before long, there was a nightly Bring Your Own Liquor party, enchanced by people from the staff who came to sing and dance for the guests.

One Angel, 1968

CHAPTER FOUR

Angels In The Dream

A family atmosphere exists amongst the staff at Napili Kai that is not common to many resorts. This attitude springs from more than simply the length of employee service, which in many cases is 15 to 20 years at Napili Kai: the atmosphere comes from caring. Perhaps the greatest evidence of this feeling is embodied in the Napili Kai Foundation.

When the Napili Kai Beach Club opened its doors in 1962, the 12-room resort employed two housekeepers and one gardener. It so happened that the housekeepers each had a couple of young daughters and that the gardener had a five-year-old granddaughter.

Guests gathered in the cabana in the balmy evenings to enjoy each other's company and were entertained by the housekeepers' and gardener's informal ukulele-playing and singing. Often, the youngsters accompanied their elders and enchanted the guests with impromptu hulas. A custom was being born although no one noticed at the time. As the resort expanded over the next few years, so did the staff... and the number of young children at this evening gathering. Such evenings were never planned; rather, they were subject to the whim of the housekeepers.

By the time the 32-room Honolua Wing opened, the cabana was too small to accommodate these pleasureable occasions. Moving the gatherings to The Teahouse of the Maui Moon, which had a large deck, triggered an idea: why not put on a show? The housekeepers were both delighted and enthusiastic!

Enter the bureaucracy which dictated that such occasions could not be done by whim as they would interfere with schoolwork! So, the entertainment was scheduled for Friday nights, a pattern which pleased everyone and has continued into the present day. Since the restaurant's deck was in the open air, everyone prayed for good weather on Friday nights!

There were lots of staff children by this time, and the show grew into quite an event. Payment was never involved: the event was simply something the housekeepers wanted to do. They were rightfully proud of their offspring and the children's entertainment prowess. The housekeepers were good musicians and singers too and, even if off-key in spots, were totally enchanting to the guests.

Friday nights rolled along in this fashion until 1965, when a Canadian guest asked Jack,

"What do you do in return for all of this?"

His question started Jack, Marg, and Dorothy thinking. Momentum gathered. Jack and Marg successfully petitioned the Internal Revenue Service for a non-profit, tax-exempt body: thus, the Napili Kai Foundation was born and each member of the staff of Napili Kai Beach Club was automatically a member of the Foundation. From this membership, a board of directors was formed. This board, along with the Millars, solicited donations to enable the hiring of teachers for the youngsters. The goal of the Foundation was to perpetuate Hawaiiana: to instruct the children in the Hawaiian culture and arts, and to instill in the children a pride in their ancestry.

That was an admirable and valuable goal because, in the 1960s, the attitude amongst many of Hawaii's youth was negative toward their own background and typified in the following remark: "It's so much better on the mainland than it is over here!" As soon as a good young dancer qualified, he or she would seek a job with a revue on the mainland. Jack's opinion was that, sadly, many young people shunned all of the lovely Hawaiian they should have assimilated growing up in the Islands. The Millars wanted to teach the youngsters to be proud of their legacy.

Hiring teachers was a formidable task since the Millars, being newcomers to Hawaii, did not know much about the Hawaiians' heritage or what the different dances meant. The board of directors, being unfamiliar with the hiring of teachers, was not much help. And, the job did not end with simply finding a teacher! Funds for costumes and salaries for additional teachers had to be managed. Finally, Dorothy sought to hire a teacher who could oversee the additional hiring. A succession of teachers passed through Napili Kai's doors until Kuulei Lay was hired. Happily, Kuulei's association with the Foundation lasted 11 years.

Kuulei had three young sons and a daughter who could become Foundation members. Also, her husband and eldest son were interested in the project. Kuulei, a talented hula dancer and teacher, is the person who is responsible for developing the Foundation to its present format.

As time progressed the board found that simply teaching the children was not enough. The challenge was to continually stimulate the child's interest. The idea to organize trips to the other islands appealed to the board; it seemed an excellent way to show the youngsters a part of their heritage and to provide an incentive which would sustain their enthusiasm. The idea worked!

Initially, the cost of interisland travel was too high to allow such an excursion but, eventually, a trip to Lanai was planned. All of the children and two or three Napili Kai shareholders travelled to Lanai on the *Coral Sea,* a boat which operated out of the Lahaina harbor. The sea was rough that morning, and almost everyone on board got sick.

One such person happened to be a doctor. He was stretched out—feeling horribly uncomfortable—and rolling around on the deck when an older child came to him and said,

"We have some sick children. Could you come take a look?"

He handed her some Dramamine tablets and replied, "I'm sorry. I don't make housecalls on board ship !"

The group arrived feeling shaky; but, once ashore at Manele Bay, everyone revived and had a wonderful day. The mothers had planned the food, which the Foundation had purchased, and the menu included a variety of ethnic dishes. At sunset, the *Coral Sea* returned to transport the group back to Maui. The day had been full of fun with lots of singing and ukulele-playing, and news of the day spread quickly by word-of-mouth.

Soon, the Foundation was beseiged by more aspirants for membership than it could handle! The decision was made that the membership would have to be limited to 36 children because the donation income the Foundation projected would probably not be enough to do a good job for more. Great care was taken in accepting students in that the Foundation had had some experience with children who joined the group, not for their own interest, but because their mothers wanted them to have the lessons or use the Foundation as a babysitting service. The Foundation was only interested in acquiring students who wanted to excel and perhaps be Hawaii's future professionals.

In 1970, the layout of the Teahouse was reconsidered with the Foundation in mind, and it was decided to construct a stage for the Friday night performances. The platform was designed so that the area could be used for dining except on show nights, when the barriers would be removed and the overhead and footlights would be turned on. The lava rock wall provides a natural backdrop for the dancers.

While aiming to look professional, performers strive to resemble their ancestors. Make-up is prohibited, and costumes are as authentic as possible. The Foundation supplies the ti leaves, and each child learns to make his or her own skirt.

Initially, the Foundation paid ten cents for each ti leaf, and the skirt expense was considerable. The larger girls used three to four times as many leaves in their skirts as did the skinnier children! Consequently, a child learned to preserve

When the Tea House was built, the kids performed on the deck. This picture was taken after a renovation about 1938.

his or her skirt by wetting down the skirt after the performance, rolling it up in newspaper, and refrigerating the bundle.
That way, the skirt's life extended to a month!

Time passed, and when the Foundation felt there was
enough money for further interisland trips for the children, a
routine developed of visiting Honolulu shortly before Christmas. The group would fly to Honolulu, stay in a hotel, and
visit Castle Park, Sea Life Park, and Paradise Park in Manoa
Valley. Once, the group visited The Polynesian Cultural
Center in Laie, and when the people learned the Foundation
was there, they asked the children to perform some dances
onstage. It was truly an exciting experience for the
youngsters.

The purpose of the visits exceeded simply having fun,
however. Performances were scheduled for the retarded
children at the Waimanu Home, for the crippled children in

We didn't know it could rain so Christmas dinner for guests was held on
the front lawn of the Lahaina Wing, 1963.

Shriners' Hospital, and for the elderly in the Lunalilo Home because the Foundation directors wanted to give the children a chance to share their talents with people less fortunate than they. Also, the directors hoped the Foundation children would realize their own good fortune when they realized they had healthy, coordinated, functioning bodies—a lesson the directors could not convey in words to the children.

One of the most satisfying times was visiting the Lunalilo Home. The older people were so enraptured and delighted with the performance that many of the elderly people stood up and danced in the aisles, joining the children in many of the pieces. The youngsters were greatly amused by this, but the greater pleasure undoubtedly belonged to the old folks, who were happily reminded of the music in their youth.

The last stop on these Honolulu excursions is always the Ala Moana Shopping Center. Younger children are entrusted to the care of the older youths, and they leave the chartered bus with strict instructions on when to return. The Foundation always gives the children money for breakfast and learns later that the money invariably was spent on ice cream or a gift! From Ala Moana, the group buses to the Honolulu Airport and flies back to Kahului, where a group of families eagerly awaits the children. Such a two-night excursion for 40 people costs close to $5,000.

Another hefty expenditure is wardrobe. In order to keep the costumes in good condition, skilled seamstresses are needed. New costumes are always in demand—children grow older and leave the group, and the incoming members seem always to be of a different shape!

So, whereas the Foundation's initial budget was $20,000, it has escalated over the years, and now, in 1985, hovers in the $50,000 range. The numbers prove that the Foundation has indeed become a viable entity.

Because of the costs of running this non-profit foundation, money is solicited continually. The principal donors are the guests who attend the Friday night performances and leave donations in the envelopes which are placed on the tables. The Napili Kai management and staff are gratified

The Foundation performing on the special stage built for the 10th

that the people who attend the show understand the cost of lessons and opportunities for children and are so generous in the amounts of the donations.

In 1977, an opportunity arose which caused great excitement for Foundation members. Dorothy Millar met with her friend, Virginia Zamboni, who was the director of special events at St. John's Hospital & Care Center in Santa Monica, California. St. John's Center for Child Study deals with child abuse and retardation. The two women thought it would be wonderful to get the children in both places together. So, the announcement was made: the Napili Kai Foundation was going to the mainland!

Letters soliciting funds were mailed, and an angel appeared in the form of the Ahmanson Foundation in Los Angeles, which underwrote the roundtrip airline tickets for the group. Without the generous help of this foundation, the trip would not have been possible since the Napili Foundation's funds were inadequate.

Anniversary party, 1970.

The hardest part of the planning was choosing which of the children would go on the trip — only 20 youngsters could go. It was a terribly difficult decision because the directors wished to take the seniors, who would soon be leaving the Foundation, and some of the smallest dancers, who were truly heart stealers! The task fell to Kuulei Lay, who selected the best 20 dancers. Plans solidified!

The night of December 9, 1978, saw Dorothy Millar, who had gone ahead to insure a smooth operation, awaiting the group's arrival at the Los Angeles Airport. The temperature was in the low 30s, and the 'Hawaiians' were wearing only their matching cotton aloha shirts and muumuus. One can imagine the 20 young people and the seven adults, shivering and chattering excitedly while they awaited their baggage!

Virginia was Dottie's liason in Los Angeles and was invaluable in helping with the plans. Virginia had solicited a bus and driver for the nine-day trip, and the bus doubled as a dressing room. Costumes were hanging all over the inside of the bus, and it was a sight to behold!

Many of the youngsters had never been to the mainland before and were awed by the newness of the experience. They gawked and chattered as they drove past billboards and negotiated congested freeways. Likewise, the 'Hawaiian' chaperones had fun! For Dorothy, however, not being as relaxed as her Hawaiian companions, the adventure was "nightmarish fun!"

She spent much of her time checking to make sure everyone was where he or she was supposed to be. Dorothy would enter the lobby of the Miramar Hotel and spy comic books strewn on sofas or a pair of shoes—one shoe here, one shoe there!—which, undoubtedly, belonged to one of the children. As far as the Napili Foundation youngsters were concerned, the Miramar Lobby was their own living room!

Dorothy and the other chaperones counted noses nightly. After one such bedcheck, Dorothy doubled back. She stepped into the elevator, only to find one of the little girls in her nightgown, hugging her pillow, sneaking to another girl's room so that they could be together. Later, Dorothy remarked,

"I guess if you have kids, you are used to this; but, for me, it was harrassing at the time! But, I wouldn't have changed or missed it!"

The Napili Foundation was awhirl with activities and excitement. On the day that the Foundation arrived, the mayor of Santa Monica, Donna Swink, declared the week Aloha Week in her city. Arrangements were made to take the group to Knotts Berry Farm—where the children danced, to Universal Studios, and to *Disneyland*.

The afternoon at Knotts Berry Farm was quite chilly, and the children were real troopers as they performed with bare midriffs in their usual costumes. At the beginning of the show, there was a small audience; but, by the end of the performance, a couple of hundred people were applauding! The children were thrilled by this warm reception and felt a real sense of being performers.

Pat and Dick Heppe, Napili Kai shareholders who live atop a steep hill in Pasadena, had graciously extended a dinner invitation to the group. The hill, however, proved too much for the bus, so the kids had to walk a couple of blocks up the curving road. This they accomplished, carolling all the way. The singing was not lost on the neighbors as they all came out to hear "Mele Kalikimaka" sung on the return walk. After a wonderful meal, Dick astounded the children by turning on his electric piano. They were absolutely fascinated that music could come from the piano without anyone sitting at it! They had never heard of such a magical piano that could play music off rolls.

The main purpose of the trip, however, was to perform— and, perform the children did! On the big day, a rehearsal took place after breakfast at St. John's Hospital. Then, the show began at 1:30 p.m.

From the Hospital, the Foundation group bussed to the 2600-seat Santa Monica Civic Auditorium, where a two-hour performance for Mr and Mrs. Lawrence Welk was scheduled. A Tahitian number began the show and amazed Lawrence Welk. The look on his face was unchanged during the entire performance; and, afterwards, he asked if he could tape the children for his show. Alas, the taping could only be done in his studio on a Tuesday. Since the group would not be there for another Tuesday, taping was impossible, and the members could only hope for a future opportunity.

The children danced that afternoon in front of an audience of approximately one thousand people and were wonderful. What a difference from performing before the smaller audiences the children had known in Hawaii!

The group also performed at the British consul general's home, and the experience was another exciting opportunity for them. The last day—Saturday—was devoted to sightseeing, shopping, and a wind-up banquet in Chinatown. Sunday morning was departure time, and what a time it was! Somehow, the 42 pieces of luggage with which the group had arrived had multiplied to 76 pieces! At the Los Angeles

In the Tea House before a stage was built, early '70s.

Airport, it took a full hour to tag and unload the bags! Finally, the excited and exhausted group was aboard the plane and homeward bound after a trip made possible through the generosity of so many individuals.

Napili's own shareholders have been wonderful supporters of the Foundation. Once, in 1980, several women shareholders decided to stage a 'flea market' as a fundraiser. The public was invited to the resort, where stalls had been put up around the grounds. All merchandise was new, and many items, including homemade jams and jellies, were suitable for Christmas gifts. The women raised $4,500 that day, a substantial contribution to the Foundation's coffer.

1980 brought change to the Foundation. Napili Kai enjoyed a high rate of returning guests—most of whom had

seen the show. The Foundation wanted to prevent the dancers from becoming bored with the routines so the decision was reached to introduce new dances. At that point, Kuulei Lay turned to other endeavors, and the Napili Foundation hired Kathy Ralar, a niece of Emma Sharpe.

Sharpe, the matriarch of Hawaiiana on Maui and a renowned hula dancer and teacher, has been a great inspiration to the Foundation. The Foundation is also indebted to Jimmy Gregg, a music teacher at Lahainaluna School and an engineer with Pioneer Mill. Along with Gregg, Emma Sharpe did many things to guide the destiny of the Foundation.

Kathy, then 21 years old, was an accomplished dancer who wanted to teach and to have her own show. Because of her youth, she had a fresh outlook and attracted a new wave of boys and girls who wanted to join the group. Kathy changed the attitude of many mothers, who had formerly viewed the Foundation experience as a babysitting service, to one involving their participation. Since Kathy's hiring, the mothers have raised funds for the group by having bake sales and car washes. The parental involvement is a satisfying aspect to the directors.

Kathy, in three or four years, established the show as one of the most popular shows on Maui. Unfortunately, attendance is limited since the show is restricted to one Friday night performance at the Sea House Restaurant (formerly the Teahouse of the Maui Moon), where tables are booked primarily for house guests. However, the Foundation does perform for the American Cancer Society and the Easter Seals Society because the directors feel those occasions offer ways of sharing for a worthy cause.

The Foundation children must leave the group when they reach the age of 18. Many of them have gone to the mainland and are professionals in Hawaiian-type shows and nightclub acts, and one youth became a teacher at the Polynesian Cultural Center on Oahu. The Millars have been gratified to see one of the 'graduates' performing in a show in other Maui hotels. It would appear that, as hoped, the Foundation has become a teaching ground for Hawaiian music and dancing.

The Foundation's reputation continued to grow, and more donations were received. Finally, in response to repeated inquiries from mainland people, the Foundation announced another trip to the West Coast would take place in 1984.

Plans were finalized, a whole new wardrobe was assembled, and the group was scheduled to leave on June 7, 1984. Tragedy struck on May 26th in the guise of a fire! Fortunately for the hotel, the fire was contained in the basement of the Aloha Wing; but, unfortunately for the Foundation, that wing was where the costumes were kept!

Only some of the Tahitian skirts which happened to be undergoing repair elsewhere were spared. All of the satin gowns were ruined! It appeared that the trip would have to be

Napili Kai Foundation boys in the early '70s.

cancelled.

But, Kathy Ralar was determined that nothing would spoil the mainland plans! She rallied all of the mothers together for a 'sew-in'; and, in one week, they had accomplished what had seemed impossible. The costumes were finished. Originally, it had taken months to select the material and pick the styles; but, when speed was of utmost importance, everyone had pitched in and finished the job. The accomplishment was a tribute to Kathy's ingenuity and the ability and desire of the mothers.

The process of retrieving 45 pieces of luggage in Los Angeles, including crates with costumes and instruments, was exhausting. Along with that lengthy task, Dorothy had to deal with the police, who were hassling the group and their waiting bus. One, tiny suitcase belonging to one of the

Foundation adults, early '70s.

youngest boys in the group was lost, and the child was in
tears. Although it was small enough to fit under the plane
seat, he had checked his one piece of baggage. Needless to
say, he was absolutely distraught. Dorothy returned to the
airport the next morning and, happily, located the lost piece
much to his relief!

Once again, the Foundation stayed at the Sheraton
Miramar in Santa Monica. The hotel was wonderful to the
members, even to the extent of refrigerating the dancers' ti
leaf skirts each evening. Every morning, the children gathered next to the pool and strung their plumeria leis while the
group's musicians stummed their guitars. During the stay,
26,000 plumeria blossoms—flown in through the courtesy of
United Airlines—were used! The lei-making sessions were a
source of great entertainment for other Miramar guests!

This second trip to California featured highlights like
Disneyland, Universal Studios, and a tour of the *Spruce
Goose* and the *Queen Mary*. But, since the purpose of the trip
was to raise money, more performances had been arranged
than on the previous trip. The Foundation perfomed publicly
at the Disneyland Hotel, privately for the Wrather Corpora-

tion—owner of that hotel—on the Queen Mary, and at the Kona Hawaii Restaurant in Santa Ana, where the local Hawaiian club turned out in force!

Gerald Ishibashi, the owner of the restaurant, was somewhat nervous about the appearance of an unknown group—especially since the well-known Society of Seven had just finished a gig there. However, Gerald was so impressed with the Foundation that afterwards he extended an open invitation to the group for a return visit and made a hefty donation to the "Children For Children' fund.

The most important performance took place the following day at the St. John's Hospital & Care Center. The north lawn of the hospital was turned into a theatre, complete with a stage, sound equipment, wind screens, and T.V. cameras, and the performance was televised for a Los Angeles Saturday morning show, "L.A.–A.M." Dorothy was presented with commendations for the Foundation from the mayor of Santa Monica and from a gentleman, Herb McRoy, representing the County of Los Angeles. These commendations are displayed against the Napili Kai Beach Club's lobby wall.

An exhilarated group of youngsters returned to the Los Angeles Airport to travel home. The children didn't really want to leave California; but, at the same time, they were eager to relate their adventures to their parents and friends! As always, the group was strikingly attractive in matching outfits—the girls in muumuus sewn from Napili Kai Beach Club material, and the boys in matching aloha shirts with white or black pants. They also sang a refrain, composed two years ago by Kathy Ralar, Phyllis Ross, and one of the mothers, which has become quite popular with the youngsters. In fact, they sing it whenever they enter or exit a restaurant or an airport!

NAPILI KAI FOUNDATION SONG
We are the keikis of Hawaii Nei
Proud to share our joy and love today

Smiling faces, graceful hands
Telling stories of our land.

We all will sing and dance for you
Give a lei or two
Make you laugh and smile
Glad you stayed a while
So, come again and see
Our group in harmony.
We are Napili Kai Foundation.

There is an incentive for the children to improve their skills. In October or November, the Foundation invites an odd variety of professional people with expertise in Hawaii-ana—perhaps writers of Hawaiian songs or dancers—to judge a show. Such judges are sought who have no connection to any of the children.

Rules exist for grading, and the dancers are judged on: their interpretation of the dance, their technical ability, and their ability to project their personality to the audience. Since the children dance Tahitian, Maori, Samoan, and Hawaiian hulas, the instructors in those areas will mark the dancers on their willingness to learn and how they get along with companions in the group.

At the Christmas show, awards are presented. A first prize and a runner-up ward is given in each of the divisions which are dictated by age and sex. An overall prize is also given. In 1984, a seven-year old received that honor!

Such a monetary prize is the only instance in which a child receives money from the Foundation. At the Christmas party, the children are also given Christmas stockings and gift certificates for clothing which are purchased from local stores where the children shop.

Unfortunately, the 1984 California trip's expenses exceeded the donations which were received so that the Foundation could not present St. John's Hospital & Care Center with any money. Since the entire trip had been

View over the Friendship Fountain.

designed with such a gift in mind and that end had not been possible, the Foundation, at its next meeting, decided to make a $5,000 donation to the Child Study Center.

Virginia Zamboni arranged for Dorothy to present that donation at a celebrity cocktail party, which was occasioned by the Jimmy Stewart Marathon (a 10-K run), at the Beverly Wilshire Hotel. So, in January, 1985, Dorothy Millar presented the $5,000 check on behalf of the Foundation to Jimmy Stewart and his assistant, Robert Wagner. When Dorothy was introduced as 'the woman with 42 children,' Jimmy Stewart gasped! He recovered quickly, and, in his lovely drawl, asked if she had any twins among them?

Celebrity Cocktail Party. Dot presents Jimmy Stewart and Bob Wagner with $5000 on behalf of the Napili Kai Foundation, January 1985.

Dorothy graciously replied that she belonged to a foundation and presented the check with the love, aloha, and sincere good wishes from all the Foundation children to the children for whom he was having the marathon.

Upon leaving the party, Dorothy was asked when the Foundation might return as a group.

"If we had the money, we'd be here tomorrow," she responded, "because our children in the Foundation want to share."

The Foundation youngsters take their membership seriously. The criteria for performing on a Friday night is that a child attend the twice-weekly rehearsals, which increase to daily sessions if something special is on the agenda. The show is done every Friday night unless the group is off-island; although, recently it was decided to give the children a short break in early December. The members must respect a strict code of behavior which prohibits smoking, drinking, and drugs.

The youngsters acquire poise through their show experience. An incident is recalled when a fourteen-year-old girl's skirt dropped to her ankles while she was dancing a Tahitian

Picture of Napili Kai Foundation kids, 1983.

hula. She immediately picked it up, walked offstage quickly, repinned it, and returned to continue the show.

When Kathy Ralar is unable to emcee the weekly performance, Linda Iwamoto, the Foundation's current president and Napili Kai Beach Club's reservations manager, takes over Kathy's duty. Linda, mother of five children, is an extraordinary woman of Japanese ancestry with an abundance of Hawaiian aloha and ability. She is a gorgeous hula dancer who teaches for Emma Sharpe and dances in Emma's show, and has been an important person to the Foundation.

Another person to whom the Foundation is indebted is Douglas Tihada, manager of the Sea House Restaurant, who was the original president of the Foundation and held that position for many years. Doug has a lovely voice and used to sing onstage, ending the show with "Hawaii Pono'i," the Hawaiian national anthem.

1985 is the Foundation's 20th year, and many of the women shareholders decided to try once more to raise money for the organization. They have worked on the plans for a year and have planned a huge marketplace for November

14th. The event will feature a show under a tent, a silent auction, baked goods, many things for sale, and a raffle for which 20,000 tickets are being sold.

The Foundation is a worthwhile, loving entity—something the Millars feel is the envy of some people who wanted to do something like it but never got around to doing it. It keeps the children off the streets and out of trouble, while teaching them their history, the Hawaiian language, the flora and fauna, and the skills associated with the Hawaiian arts. The Foundation gives a child an experience: something that no one can take away from the child and of which the child can always be proud.

Opposite page: Lahaina parking lot, 1963-64.

A sign of the times. Story on page 67.

CHAPTER FIVE

Down Came Baby, Mountainside And All

In 1964, an arrangement was made to convert the agreement on the one-and-a-half-acre parcel of land between the Lahaina and Honolua Wings from lease to purchase. This was also the site of the cottage and a large trapezoidal swimming pool which exist there today.

The corporation had agreed to a selling price of $1.25 per square foot and approached the bank for a loan. Then, bank appraisers set a value of $.35 per square foot on the land. Since the bank felt Napili Kai had agreed on a ridiculously high price, they were not especially interested in loaning Napili Kai money. Today, that property would market between $25 and $30 per square foot.

Jack also entered negotiations in 1964 to acquire a long-term lease on another property, sensing its importance in future expansion. That land now supports the Aloha Wing, tennis court and shop, and the maintainance area.

It was a difficult time for management as Jack kept returning to the shareholders with requests for additional monies. Some of the board members were unhappy with management's plans and projections. They felt that expansion was rash since the company was still operating at a loss. The outcome of the discord was that Jack took the leases in his own name. Later, board members changed, and newcomers were happy to accept the leases in the name of Napili Kai, Ltd.

A crisis occurred in 1964 that impacted the future of the resort. The largest mango orchard in the world was planted on the hillside above Napili Bay. The plantation decided to put the land into pineapple production. This meant that the big old trees were cut down, and their stumps were dug out of the ground. A tractor crisscrossed the acreage with a deep one-pronged plow to dig out the underground rock which had the effect of loosening the ground.

Jack feared that an awful mass of red mud could slide down the hill in a heavy rain and voiced his concern. His frustration mounted as he spoke to people and found that while they were sympathetic, his fears fell on deaf ears. Finally, he persuaded the U. S. Soil Conservation Service to call a meeting of plantation and county people in October, 1963. Again, Jack found that although they were nice to him, little concern was paid to his worries.

December, 1964, brought lovely days accompanied by ten nights of steady light rain. Soon, the resort grounds were mushy and soggy. The days got darker and darker, until one Saturday evening 11 inches of rain poured down from the sky in two hours' time. Guests had to be moved to the upper floors because of the amount of muddy water passing through the buildings. Thigh-deep water ran between the Lahaina and Honolua Wings.

Ruth Nettleship phoned Jack from the office to tell him that she and her son were nearly swept away by the torrent of thick mud when they tried to cross between the two buildings and that the muddy water was pouring down over the tops of the toilets. Afterwards, crossings were attempted only if three or four people were there to hold onto each other. Pieces of the concrete wall which had been at the back of the property had been carried to the oceanfront, and cars in the hotel parking lot smashed against each other.

The debris which accompanied the water was disgusting. Drowned rats were in the torrent, and centipedes and scorpions were found crawling in clothes.

As the rain increased and the water level rose, Margaret and Dottie thought they should try to save the towels, Kleenex, and toilet paper. So, the two women made their way to the housekeeping department, only to find the cupboards

The beach cabana after the first night of flooding.

with supplies already underwater! The water rose, and soon
the maids' refrigerator was floating.

"Open the door and sink it," exclaimed Margaret!

Dottie refused, thinking for some crazy reason that it was
important to save the food in it.

The women unplugged the appliance, suffering only a
few minor shocks, finally opened its door, and left the
area.

Dorothy put the reservations charts and the financial
books into garbage cans and floated them next door to the
Mauian. One of the guests had run back to her room to get her
wig and in so doing had slipped and broken her leg. Dotty
floated her to the Mauian on a surfboard.

By about two oclock a.m. guests were safe in the upstairs
rooms. Poor Marg had to content with a drunk, an over-
weight fellow, who went downstairs repeatedly to check on
the flooding; all she could do was pull him upstairs again. All

downstairs doors were wide open so that the water could pass through the building. Being the lowest property in that area, water came at the resort from all inland directions. Even though the rain had stopped by 2 a.m., the mud was above knee level.

When Margaret opened the door to their cottage, she was hit by a suitcase, shoes, and Christmas presents which had been under the tree—all of which floated inside the house. The two poodles and one puppy were nervously perched atop a sofa which was floating in the living room. The exhausted and muddy Millars lay down on their wet beds with nothing more they could do until the dawn brought light.

The Sunday morning scene was one of absolute desolation. There was red mud as far as one could see. The ground in front of the Lahaina Wing had been torn out, and what remained of the cabana was undermined by at least six feet. The swimming pool was full of mud, and the river had gorged a channel between the restaurant and the Honolua Wing, isolating the Teahouse. The kiawe trees which grew along the beach had disappeared overnight. Two or three cars had been

After the second night, showing the continuing erosion of beach.

carried into the ocean; and, where the ocean had been 10 feet deep, it was now possible to walk on the mud to the reef which was only three to four inches below the water.

The road was under 8–10 inches of mud so that only a tractor could pass on it, and the electricity was off. County crews plowed out the road that day so that there was access past the resort and winched the cars out of the parking lot to the road with huge cables.

The sky glowered all day that Sunday. More rain was forecast, and many of the guests were nervous. Tony de Jetley, manager of The Royal Lahaina Resort, generously offered to accommodate Napili guests at the same rates they were paying at Napili. Half of the guests accepted the offer. The other half, excited by their involvement in a disaster, opted to stay.

Reverend John Kukahiko replaced his church service with an appeal to his congregation to go home for shovels and help dig out Napili Kai. People even came from Kula to shovel out the rooms—lines of cars of helpers stretched back for nearly half a mile.

The greatest challenge was to create a defense against further damage in case another storm were to come that night. Through the help of the Pacific Flight Service, then the only commuter airline out of Kaanapali, and the Maui highway department, Napili Kai was able to purchase sandbags from the Honolulu Corps of Engineers. Joe Jones flew a full load of the bags over in his Beechcraft.

Three thousand sandbags guarded the upper perimeter of the property by Sunday night. Nine inches more rain fell that night, followed by 10 inches more on Monday, giving Napili Kai a total of 30 inches in a three-day period.

The assistance which came from the community was both invaluable and touching. Danny Fong of Fong Construction donated a big tractor that Monday to excavate an old, unused right-of-way in hope of facilitating drainage which ran through the resort's property. Unfortunately, a neighbor whose property abutted this easement went to court and persuaded the judge to issue a temporary injunction against Napili Kai, halting further excavation of this right-of-way. Napili Kai's only recourse was to wait until February for a court date when they could appeal this order—which they lost. Two years passed before the appeal to the Supreme

Court of Hawaii could be heard—that court issued a judgement rescinding the lower court's decision. But, during that interval, Napili Kai could not work on the right-of-way.

Eventually, Jack persuaded the County of Maui to take over the right-of-way as a water easement—not a road. Jack agreed to grass and maintain it in an attractive condition, and this plan has worked out to everyone's advantage over the ensuing years.

Pioneer Mill dispatched a full shift, 60–70 workers, and equipment to Napili Kai's aid. Maui Land and Pineapple Company sent a full crew and two tractors to the resort to restore the beachfront. All of the beds, mattresses, carpets, and some of the furniture from the lower floors of both wings were thrown into the hole in front of the Lahaina Wing and were covered up by the bulldozers. Likewise, the big kiawes which had been uprooted were re-erected with the help of the bulldozers.

Watching the bulldozers working on what remained of the beach was most interesting. A 10-foot cliff had been created at the edge of the property by the undermining water action. It was as though the beach had been torn out from the rest of the property. The bulldozers ran out on the mud and pushed the mud up toward the property, forming a muddy patchwork of beach.

The Millars had to contend with the cleanup of their cottage also which was carpeted by a 12-inch layer of the gooey, red mud which stuck to the shovel when a person tried to fling the mud out the door. The problem was solved by axing holes into the floor and scraping the mud into those holes. Afterwards, the Millars covered the holes with aluminum pie plates, which were later hidden by carpeting.

Later, Jack tried to express management's thanks to the community with a full-page ad in *The Maui News* (*opposite*).

Despite the horrendous damage, humorous moments shone through the disaster. Guests were amused at seeing Ruth, barefooted and in a bathing suit, operate the front desk.

On behalf of myself and the other shareholders of NAPILI KAI BEACH CLUB I wish to publicly thank the people of Maui for their tremendous Aloha and Kokua during the three attacks of mud and water suffered by our hotel during the heavy rains. Without their tremendous co-operation we could not have survived alone.

I wish to thank first the Staff, their families and relatives for their tremendous and un-tiring efforts in not only helping to clean up but for their great effort of sand-bagging the broken walls on Sunday which helped mightily when we were hit again Sunday night.

I wish to thank the many people who helped us and offered help who we did not know personally nor know that they were here helping.

I wish to thank Mayor Eddie Tam for his prompt return from Honolulu. He personally inspected the damage and provided men and machines to help fortify the property.

The co-operation of the County through its Mayor and Board of Supervisors in provid-ing men and machines was of invaluable help.

I want to especially thank John and Mrs. Fernandez who lived in the hotel and whose prompt action with men and machines in the middle of the night on the third attack, managed to stave off the worst attack of all, which undoubtedly would have knocked over our Lahaina Building

I am especially grateful to John Stegmuller of Maui Pine who supplied endless personal effort as well as machines and who has rebuilt our beach to where it is more beautiful than ever.

The action of Tony deGentry of Royal Lahaina Hotel in housing our guests without ad ditional cost to the guest is especially appreciated.

The Kokua of Fong Construction and its mighty machines during the holiday period has earned our gratitude.

However, it is individual people such as plumbers, electricians, carpenters, neighbors and friends, who have shown us the true Spirit of Maui.

There is no question that both our main buildings would have been totally destroyed if it was not for the work done between each attack. Without the tremendous work far into the night by all concerned, the continued piling up of mud and water would have made Napili Kai totally unsalvagable.

As it is today we are back in business with all rooms occupied by wonderful guests en-joying themselves on a beautiful beach, swimming in the pool and all facilities operat-ing except, of course, the gardens.

To Joe Amaral, who spent three years of love and hard work building these beautiful gardens, I extend sympathy coupled with encouragement that in a few months it will be even more beautiful.

The Tea House of the Maui Moon is operating: Breakfast, lunch and dinner and the view from it is as magnificent as ever.

We are deeply grateful that there was no loss of life, and no fatal injuries to anyone. Near tragedy, may result in preventive measures to insure others against such disasters in the future.

We have truly learned the meaning of Aloha, and Kokua and Napili Kai is proud to be a Member of the Maui Community.

Please accept our heartfelt Mahalo Nui.

(Signed)

J. C. MILLAR

President & Managing Director
Napili Kai Beach Club

Above: Lahaina and Honolua Wings. *Opposite page:* Collage of flood pictures, poems, sketches and other humor by Herrmann family after the first flood.

Dewey, Jack and Margaret's son, had been visiting from Honolulu that weekend and tried to create merriment out of the disaster in order to keep the guests happy. So, Monday night after the Teahouse had been thoroughly stripped of carpeting and scrubbed clean, the resort hosted the famous Mud Party.

All of the guests were invited for cocktails and heavy pupus (hors d'oeuvres). Dewey composed a song, "Mud, Mud, Glorious Mud," which was uproariously sung many times over the course of the evening. The merry refrain was as follows:

"Mud, mud, glorious mud
        nothing quite like it for cooling the blood;
Follow me follow, down to the hollow—
        there we will wallow in glorious mud."

Restoration of grounds took a full year. Photo of Lahaina Wing a year later.

Several of the guests, attired in bathing suits, actually rolled in the mud—even obscuring their faces—before entering the party. It was an evening of great hilarity!

The Mud Party featured a fashion show, a performance unlike any before seen on Maui! Four guests and one Mauian were the models in the show called, "Fastidious Fashions for Fearless Mud Fighters." Models portrayed frogmen, original Hawaiian Mud Sweepers, a Teenager Mud Snorkler, and several other hilarious fashions!

The hard fact remained, however, that losses had been incurred. The ocean was muddy as far as one could see, and swimming was impossible. The cost of Napili Kai's clean-up and loss of income was estimated at $200,000, and Jack did not know where he would find that money.

Jack was most appreciative of Clifton Terry, president of the Bank of Hawaii in Honolulu, who had phoned Jack that Monday and authorized a $50,000 emergency loan. Jack dubbed Terry's gesture a stroke of aloha.

CHAPTER SIX

Rebuilding
A Waterlogged Dream

Vancouver newswriters had painted a picture of doom in reporting the flood and alarmed many of Napili Kai's prominent shareholders, who lived in Vancouver. They were not willing to invest more money in a concern they feared was a total loss. Shares in the Napili Kai corporation were then $6 per share. A five-year debenture was offered at 7½%, convertible into common shares at $2 at the end of five years, but virtually no one was interested. The word was out that Napili Kai was a disaster. Only a few small gestures from a handful of shareholders lightened the black mood.

Millar sought the opinion of a Honolulu attorney, Frank Padgett, as to whether or not Napili Kai had a claim against Maui Land and Pineapple Company because of their method of plowing the field. Padgett referred to a decision written by Oliver Wendell Holmes which stated that "if the man above took no untoward action to the man below him, he was in no way responsible for any damage that might happen from normal farming practices."

Alexander & Baldwin, which then owned Maui Land and Pineapple Company, sent a vice president to Jack who expressed their sympathy and said that if he wanted to make a case out of it, there would be no recriminations from them because they would welcome a test case due to their many similar fields and responsiblities throughout the island. Jack did not wish to take on the giant corporation and has enjoyed his pleasant relationship with them since.

As it turned out, Dr. Chipperfield, a Vancouver shareholder who was a vice president of the Napili Kai corporation for many years thereafter, Tommy Campbell, a lawyer who had been one of Jack's partners in the metal business and who was the secretary of Napili Kai for many years, and the Millars bought the majority of the debenture. With these funds and the loan from the Bank of Hawaii, Jack was able to reconstruct the property and make major changes to prevent a future occurrence. The rooms were redone, and Napili Kai was back in business!

Since the resort was unable to excavate the right-of-way and rely on it for drainage relief, a concrete wall was built around the front of the property, and a ditch was dug to run through the central part of the property. The ditch was designed to handle 500 cubic feet per second and its seaward mouth was lined in concrete.

But, disaster struck again! On an overcast February afternoon in 1965, Jack was in court in Wailuku at a hearing regarding the injunction. Dot phoned the court to say Napili Kai was having further flooding and that Jack's presence was required immediately. A huge kiawe branch had blocked the water's passage through the concrete channel. Silt had amassed behind the log, causing the water to jump the banks and roar across the lawns, ripping out sod and more of the beachfront, and the concrete mouth of the ditch had collapsed in upon itself since the water had undermined the earth around it (opposite page).

Jack requested the judge to recess the hearing and to come to Napili Kai so that the judge could see the necessity of opening the right-of-way. Meanwhile, guests Danny Ekman and Bob Cowan, were the day's heroes when they persuaded guests to take the poolside sunboards, find some planks, and redirect the enormous flow of water back toward the ditch and away from the cabana. The branch was far too large to move. More sandbags were put into place.

The judge was impressed by the downpour and desolation. But, weeks later, he entered his verdict upholding the injunction and ordering Napili Kai to fill in the right-of-way.

When the work began on rebuilding the 8 feet wide and 6

feet deep concrete-lined ditch, the engineers discovered that the ditch ran uphill towards the ocean! In fact, this very expensive drainage project was 18 inches higher at the ocean than at its backside. Management was furious: no wonder it didn't empty itself!

Redoing the ditch was a major undertaking. Management realized that the construction noise would be horrendous on

the day that the jackhammers were scheduled to work, so Napili Kai planned a day-long picnic to which all guests were invited. The cooperation of the guests was wonderful: all guests responded favorably and were transported in plush, air-conditioned busses to Kalama Park in Kihei, where they were treated to lunch, liquor, and games. A wonderful and lavish time had been created by the Beach Club. Upon returning, all the guests hastened to inspect the now deepened waterway.

Normalcy crept back into life at Napili Kai over the next few weeks, but scars remained. Napili Kai's corner of the bay drains 625 acres of fields, and when a cloudburst occurs, an incredible volume of water rushes to the bay. One estimate was 2200 cubic feet per second. Twenty- to 30-foot wide arroyos striped the fields, and one engineer estimated that

117,000 cubic yards of mud had gone through Napili Kai! Small wonder that Napili Kai acquired the stigma of being a river bottom with a resort in it! It was at this time that, after seeing photographs of the devastation, the owners of the land which was under the Teahouse and the Honolua Wing offered to sell the property to Napili Kai at $4 a square foot.

After the flood, Maui Land and Pineapple Company and several engineers met to investigate the possibility of thwarting future devastation in the event of another deluge. There was an old railway embankment up in the pineapple fields where trains used to load the pineapples from Pineapple Hill to take to the Lahaina cannery. The railway fell into disuse when the Lahaina cannery disbanded, and pineapples were trucked to the central cannery in Kahului.

The embankment ran across an enormous gulch which drained about 600 higher acres into the bay. The engineers suggested setting up a device in the gulch which would hold back 20 feet of water on the upper side of the embankment. The device would also retain silt, which would be trucked out in summer and used for topsoil. The engineers put a 20- by 6-foot diameter stand pipe which connected to the culvert under the embankment. The idea was to hold back the water during a cloudburst, then open the valve at the bottom and let the water out slowly. The device worked well for about two years.

On March 17, 1967 Jack and Dorothy were in Honolulu discussing the financing of the would-be development of the Aloha Wing with the bank when news reached them that severe flooding was occurring in Napili Bay. They raced to the airport and caught the day's last flight to Kaanapali—only to be greeted in Napili by another disaster scene!

A cloudburst had let down 7 inches of rain within an hour, and the plantation had phoned Margaret to say that the dam had overflowed and that there was no further relief for Napili Kai. In the sudden storm, the stress was so great that the culvert under the dam collapsed, letting the held-back water breach the dam. Margaret and her sister-in-law, Phyllis, who had immediately left the cottage to alert and move the guests,

were walking across the putting green through 6 inches of water when they saw a four-foot high wave of water coming toward them on its path to the bay! They grabbed ahold of some oleander bushes and were rescued by a boy on a surfboard! Marg's brother, who had also accompanied her, scrambled up a tree in time to escape the wave.

Two-hundred million gallons of water stormed through Napili Kai, carrying many branches and boulders. Some of the rocks were half the size of an automobile! Several cars were picked up by the rushing water and carried into the ocean. One such car belonged to Paddy Jacobsen, the front

office manager; it was parked on the reef!

Another car, which was stranded inside the reef, belonged to a rental agency—which demanded that the renter continue paying rent for the car since it hadn't been returned! Still another car went across the reef, losing its hubcaps on its coral path. All of the hubcaps were found, but there was never a trace of the car again!

This flood washed out all of the new planting which had been undertaken after the 1965 flooding. The beach underwent further erosion, and mud was everywhere. At one point, the assistant manager of the Teahouse rushed across the knee-deep mud to help a guest; and, suddenly, the manager disappeared! He had fallen into the swimming pool which was obscured under the muddy water level.

The odorous mud stayed around Napili Kai for a pitifully long time. Fertilizer from the pineapple fields was in the soil and created a horrible stench. Since the office was inundated by the muddy water, all of the files, records, documents, maps, blueprints, and financial statements were soaked and contaminated by the smell. Today, Jack still finds mud interleafed between some of the sheets of important papers in his desk!

Clothing, suitcases, books, and paintings were ruined by the stench also and had to be thrown away. Napili Kai was haunted by the odor for years!

However, in Margaret's words,

"Although the properties were inundated with mud, sticks, branches, rocks, centipedes, scorpions, and unwanted debris, Nature wouldn't be in character if some good things weren't provided."

Those good things were kukui nuts, which had been washed down from the mountains. The nuts sprouted out of the mud and grew rapidly, and Jack had many of the seedlings put in pots. Later, these trees were planted along the roadside from the Lahaina entrance to the Aloha Wing. The kukui (candlenut) tree was significant to the Hawaiians in that its oily kernel was used for lighting purposes, and its bark had tanning properties which helped to preserve fishnets. Also, the kukui was used medicinally.

CHAPTER SEVEN

Rebuilding Again

The next five years were difficult for Napili Kai. After this third flood, people decided that the resort was situated in the middle of a flood channel, and this unfortunate reputation once again frustrated Jack's financing efforts. Luckily, the insurance from Lloyds of London covered the majority of the recovery expenses of the 1967 flood. The resort could barely pay its bills and advertise.

Jack's opinion was that the salvation of the company lay in expansion: the resort needed more rooms to support its overhead and develop a profit. The hill property was virtually floodproof and seemed an ideal place to build a new wing. Furthermore, the pineapple fields had been newly contoured, and the chance of a repeat experience had been greatly reduced.

A flood gate had been built across the parking lot entrance. The drumming of rain on the Millars' tin roof now acted as an alarm to Marg and Dorothy. They would rush out into the rain, pull shut and padlock the heavy wooden emergency gate which barracaded the property from water and mud.

With the building of concrete walls and the excavating of the central concrete drainage ditch, Lloyds of London had been satisfied so continued to insure the resort. Nevertheless, the banks considered Napili Kai a flood area and refused to grant a loan to the corporation.

Jack sought assistance from the Small Business Administration; he asked for $850,000 to construct the 33-room Aloha

Wing. A deal was struck: the SBA would loan Napili Kai $500,000 on a 25-year loan if the corporation would raise the $350,000. Once more, enough shares were issued and sold to facilitate the construction of the new wing which opened in August of 1968. Due to the good will that the resort had established over the years with many of the guests and to the loyalty that had been generated amongst them, many guests became shareholders with this new issue.

As always, expansion did not occur without some frustrations. The Aloha Wing was designed to have a basement running the entire length of the building. When excavation began, instructions were given that the top 3 feet of lovely brown topsoil be scraped and left in a pile which could later be used for planting. The grey dirt under that layer was to be used later for backfill around the footings.

Jack, who had undergone knee surgery, hobbled to the site on his crutches on the morning the backfilling began. And, there was the bulldozer operator pushing the topsoil and using it for fill. Although conversation was difficult over the noise of the machine and the worker spoke pidgin, angry Jack gave instructions again and was certain that he had been understood this time. An hour later, Jack returned to check the progress of the job. A 4-foot high bank of earth greeted him. The operator had blocked Jack's entry by building himself a dirt wall around the area and had continued using the topsoil. All Jack could do was shake his crutches and scream at him!... and bring in new topsoil later at great expense!

Staffing an additional new wing was a challenge too. Margaret Millar was in charge of overseeing that the rooms were in order: that the rooms were vacuumed, lampshades unwrapped, and appliances plugged into the outlets. Two young men were assigned to help Marg, one of whom was named Fortunato. Marg gave a vacuum cleaner to him and instructed him to go from room to room, cleaning the carpets. Later, Marg made her rounds, checking the rooms. Judging from what she saw, she did not think that Fortunato had been to any of the rooms she'd checked. When she found him, he

Napili Kai Beach Club, July 1968.

was indeed vacuuming. The power was on, and the machine was making a loud noise, but Fortunato did not realize that the two pieces of equipment—the hose and the machine— needed to be attached in order to be effective!

Time passed, the resort's occupancy rate increased, and in 1965 the Millars purchased an oceanfront houselot a third of a

Old lobby in Aloha Wing, 1968.

mile from Napili Bay which faced Lanai and the magnificent
sunsets. They engaged their favorite Vancouver architect to
design a new home. The fine home was built and named
"Grayrocks." This lovely spot of rocky coast has been their
happy refuge since 1972.

CHAPTER EIGHT

The Race

This period in Napili Kai's history had bright moments. The Victoria-Maui International Race traces its origin to 1965, when three men from the Vancouver Yacht Club—Jim Innes, Lol Killam, and N. R. Ramsay—set sail from Vancouver to Maui. The trio sailed their yachts without escorts and depended on the Canadian Pacific Air flights which flew to Honolulu two or three times a week for their only reporting mechanism. Their destination was the Kahului Harbor where they had to register as entrants into the United States.

Innes's family was staying in the Lahaina Wing at Napili, anxiously awaiting Jim's arrival; and, when they learned that Jim had won the race on his yacht, "Long Gone," they were elated! Excitement was high!

Imagining a wonderful event for years to come, Jack suggested that this little race be made into an official biennial event which would alternate with the Transpacific Yacht Race! Jack contacted the mayor and the local press and invited them to a party which he hosted in the cabana for the skippers and their crews. The sailors were presented with small "Keys to Maui" by Charles C. Young, representing County Chairman Eddie Tam.

Ernest Halford, Maui member of the Hawaii Visitors Bureau, offered congratulations and all possible help for the success of the event and announced that the HVB would have a perpetual trophy for the race.

The idea was well-received, and a race charted for 1968. The concept of this race, which was to start from Victoria's

The three skippers in the first Victoria-Maui International race are pictured here with those of the crew that could be rounded up. Fourth from the left is the race winner, Jim Innes, owner and skipper of the *Long Gone*. On his left, behind dark glasses, is the owner/skipper of the *Norena of Wight,* and second from the right, in aloha shirt, is Lol Killam, skipper/owner of the *Velaris*.

gorgeous inner harbor, was stimulating. The Royal Canadian Navy would host a dinner for all of the captains in Victoria's grand old Empress Hotel and fire a sendoff salute. It promised to be quite a classy affair! Jack was commissioned to procure the trophies and did so, avoiding commercial ones.

Trophies were donated by the governor of Washington, the Vancouver Yacht Club, the City of Vancouver, the lieutenant governor of the province of British Columbia, the City of Victoria, the West Coast Commodores' Group, Maui County, *The Maui News,* and the governor of Hawaii. Most of the tropies were designed and made by an outstanding Canadian jewelry firm and were absolutely beautiful.

The 1968 Victoria-Maui International boasted 17 entries. The Lahaina Yacht Club had been formed by this time and was a great help in hosting the race although some of the parties were held at the Napili Kai Beach Club. The best part of the festivities was the big celebration in the Lahaina Prison. The occasion was quite a bash, and a good time was had by all!

The Victoria-Maui International currently enjoys between 50 and 60 entries; and, for sailors from the Northwest is the great race to Hawaii...rather than the Transpac.

One yachting anecdote which stands out in memories sprang out of the 1970 Victoria-Maui International. Lol Killam, one of the original racing trio, entered his new 76-foot fiberglass yacht, *Graybeard,* in the race. The *Graybeard,* the largest fiberglass sailboat in existence at that time, caught the wind after a few days of poor sailing; and, in one day, the *Graybeard* sailed 300 miles! She crossed the finish line about two days ahead of the other yachts.

After the race celebrations finished, Lol sailed the *Graybeard* to Napili and dropped anchor in the bay. She was a beautiful sight, floating atop the clear, blue ocean. However, the surf was building up. The crew was housed in the Honolua Wing, from where they could watch the yacht. A long line ran from an anchor beyond the reef to her bow, and another line tethered her stern to an anchor on the shore. There was room for lots of play in the lines, and she rode the surf beautifully.

The Millars hosted a party in their cottage that evening for the crew, and everyone had a merry time before retiring. Jack awoke with a start at 11 p.m., alarmed by a premonition. He shook Marg awake and told her that the *Graybeard* was loose, and he raced down to the beach. Sure enough! She was dangerously close to shore—the sea line to the *Graybeard's* anchor having been chewed by the reef—and was pitching wildly in the night!

Jack ran for the crew and summoned Lol, who was able to swim out to his yacht and climb aboard. The *Graybeard* was then about 20 feet from shore and close to the rocky area off the concrete pilings which can been seen along the shoreline. Jack trained a big searchlight from the Teahouse Restaurant onto the yacht. It was pitiful to watch her plunging wildly like a great white swan in distress. The beautiful, expensive yacht was obviously aground.

Organizing a rescue effort was no easy task since it was 11 p.m. on a Saturday night and most of the crews were celebrating in the Lahaina bars! Jack and Lol thought that if the *St. Anthony*, which was the Royal Canadian Navy tug which escorted the 30 yachts in the race, would come to Napili Bay, they could pull the *Graybeard* from its grounded position. That sounded like a great idea, but the *St. Anthony's* crew was spread throughout the Lahaina bars also!

The commodore of the Lahaina Yacht Club was a great help. He rounded up many *St. Anthony* crew members and the skipper and organized a small boat to accompany them in order to provide the Canadians with local knowledge of the waters and bay. At 2 a.m. the *St. Anthony* was in front of Napili Kai and ready to begin the rescue attempt.

An excitable crowd of perhaps 10 carloads of sailors, staff, and guests lined the beach. Everyone was shouting advice—inebriated advice, at that!—and knowing nothing about the matter at hand! A walkie talkie system linked the *Graybeard* to shore, and the question of what to do rebounded back and forth. The conversations which transpired between the crews were quite funny since most of the sailors had been called out of the Lahaina bars!

Well, the *St. Anthony*, which was a quarter of a mile from the shore, dispatched its longboat to the *Graybeard* to rig a cable between the *Graybeard* and the tug. The longboat's engine quit repeatedly, and a sailor had to row. Finally, the longboat got close enough to the *Graybeard* to secure the line. Then, the *St. Anthony* fired up her engines and pulled...but, the *Graybeard* didn't budge!

The next thought was for the *St. Anthony* to move to deeper water where she could anchor to a better bottom and use her winch, which would be more powerful than the forward thrust of her engines. So, the *St. Anthony* shifted seaward. Then, the longboat took a line from the *Graybeard* and had the other small vessel, which had escorted them to Napili from Lahaina, bring a 2500-foot wire cable from the *St. Anthony*.

At the signal, the *St. Anthony* began winching. Suddenly, great crunching and splitting sounds filled the air! Screams of 'stop!' 'stop!' broadcast through the walkie talkies! The silly, semi-inebriated longboat sailors had fastened the line from the *St. Anthony* to their stern and the line from the *Graybeard* to their bow! The longboat began to split apart and quickly disintegrated, and the sailors sobered up in the ocean!

Next, the small escort boat ran a 2-inch nylon line from the main mast of the *Graybeard* directly to the drowned cable of the *St. Anthony*. The *St. Anthony* began its winch once more. This time, the *St. Anthony* moved: but, not the *Graybeard!*

By now, a couple of hours had passed, and everyone was considerably more sober. However, the ocean was still violent. The radio conversations became more articulate, and another attempt was launched. This time, the *St. Anthony* had gotten a good bite with her anchor and had started her powerful winches. The cable lifted above the water; and, suddenly, the *Graybeard* shot out of the water like a projectile for about 150 feet until the line slackened and allowed her to settle back into the sea. There she sat... looking serene once more.

Much to everyone's surprise and delight, the *Graybeard* had not sustained as great an amount of damage as they expected. This was because her sharp keel had wedged in a sand bar rather than between rocks. Lol decided that she could be kept afloat by constant bailing and that he wanted to take her to Lahaina immediately. He left, accompanied by the small Lahaina vessel, and took the *Graybeard* from Lahaina to Honolulu where she entered drydock for a few months.

Aloha Wing opened in August of 1968.

CHAPTER NINE

The Dream Expands

Four houses, an empty lot, and a small graveyard were adjacent to the Aloha Wing on the rocky north shore of Napili Bay. The spot had been developed years before by Maui Land and Pineapple Company as a place for department heads; but, in fact, most of the places had been bought by people affiliated with Pioneer Mill. This area was a natural location for Napili Kai's expansion.

Jack was able to obtain a 55-year lease on the empty lot past the houses, and he directed a Honolulu architect to draw up plans for a new building. However, he encountered resistance for the development from some board members who were not interested in developing a parcel which was not contiguous to Napili Kai Beach Club.

Jack was undaunted, though, and personally developed the project as a condominium with the idea that persons who purchased units therein would allow Napili Kai to operate the condominum as a wing of the hotel and that the revenues would be divided in a specific fashion. The long-term agreements would be in 10-year increments; and, the refurbishing, maintainance, and management would be done the same way as the corporation rooms in the Napili Kai Beach Club.

The building was situated close to the ocean, closer than current shoreline restrictions would allow. Some units were only five feet from the cliff edge. In those suites, the noise of

Puna Point opened in 1970.

the lovely surf lapping on the rocks filled the rooms, and occupants felt like they were on a ship with Molokai and Lanai the only land in sight.

Jack, Marg, and Dot searched through a Hawaiian dictionary for a name for this development, feeling its ancient Hawaiian name was too difficult for mainlanders to pronounce, and settled on Puna Point. Puna means coral in Hawaiian, and the Millars felt it an apt name for the rocky, coral point. The task of selling these condominiums was an easy one: the Millars kept several for themselves, and shareholders and return guests purchased the others. The building was blessed upon completion and opened in 1970. Napili Kai assumed management of the building immediately and has operated in that fashion ever since. The building is a collection of suites and has proved to be an attractive investment.

Rapidly, the scene changed from one of debt to profit; and, in 1970, the corporation's tenth year, the company was worth its initial investment. Napili Kai Beach Club had recovered its losses! In fact, the books showed a $25,000 surplus which the board wished to return as a dividend to shareholders.

However, Napili Kai's contract with the SBA stated that the corporation needed the SBA's permission in order to pay a dividend; and, the SBA turned down the dividend-payment request even though the loan was in good order. The matter did not die there, though.

The board decided to have a gala celebration for the shareholders and Maui. Eleven hundred Maui residents were invited, including the staff and their families, the Maui council, school principals and teachers, lawyers, and guests from Honolulu. Mayor Elmer Cravalho emceed the event. The big pool was covered with a giant stage, and the lawns were strung with overhead lights. Five bars were set up, and tables of steaks, fried chicken, barbequed lobster tails, pupus, kalua pig, and desserts were positioned on the lawn. Two or three sailboats had brought guests to the party and were anchored in the bay. One of them, the *Allure,* was beautifully decorated with its masts set out in colored lights and added to the festive atmosphere.

Local musicians, playing a wide variety of Hawaiian

10th Anniversary party, 1970. *Above:* Son Dewar, Jack and Margaret Millar. *Below:* Happy throng watching events on the special stage that

Elmer Cravalho
crossed the "Z" pool.

Fireworks by Dot Millar
and Bob Jones.

music, roamed the lawn. People danced to the music of five bands, and the Napili Foundation performed many times that evening. Many talented performers were counted amongst the guests, and they took turns adding to the evening's revelry.

It was 4 a.m. when the last guests left the party. The night, graced by the gentle tradewinds, had been a tremendous success. The party had used most of the extra funds Napili Kai had allotted, but the Millars felt that the shareholders and the Maui community had had a great time and that anything could be accomplished from then on.

Progress continued. A group of Canadians from Edmunton made a lease arrangement with the owners of three houses which were immediately adjacent to the Aloha Wing. Interestingly, one of the houses belonged to the neighbor who years earlier had caused Napili Kai such trouble and grief over the right-of-way dispute. The Canadian group, persuaded the three owners to merge into a single unit and lease it to them so it could be developed as a condominium.

Jack was alarmed when he saw the initial plans and learned they planned to put 52 units on the property. One two-story building would run parallel to the property line with its back to the Aloha Wing all the way to the sea. Such a building would have blocked a substantial part of Napili Kai's ocean view and create a high wall along the side.

Jack contacted the Canadian group and tried to persuade them that reduced density on the site would be far more desirable, enjoying an atmosphere of green space rather than being crammed. However, they resisted Jack's persuasion since they had projected a certain profit plan based on a specific number of units. So, Jack and his fellow directors proposed to buy their lost profit if the group would agree to reduce their number of units to 37. Furthermore, the Napili Kai corporation would agree to buy 15 of the 37 units, thereby guaranteeing a floor under their project.

The buildings were built and were charming, and Napili Kai leased most of the units and operated them as part of the hotel complex, calling it the Lani Wing.

Based on the projected completion date, rooms in the Lani Wing were booked for guests in January, 1972. However, the resort was unable to hire enough workers to clean out the contractor's messy leavings. The sinks were spotted with putty, and the bathtubs were speckled with plaster; getting the rooms clean in time for the arrival of the guests seemed impossible.

Thus, "The Char Ladies" came into existence! Many shareholders were staying in the resort at the time, and the wives banded together to form a cleaning brigade under the direction of Dottie. "The Char Ladies" spent an entire week working with the hired maids and succeeded in cleaning the new wing in time for the first scheduled guests. It was quite a sight to see the diamond-bedecked hands don long gloves and clean the toilets! Since then, the women have met annually for a Char Ladies' Luncheon, and the good times of fun and laughter have continued.

The Char Ladies exemplified the wonderful spirit of camaraderie which has always been a part of Napili Kai. This atmosphere traces back to the time before the Teahouse of the Maui Moon existed. At that time, the resort was so small that one guest, a woman from Vancouver named Mary Kenmuir, began making coffee in her kitchenette and bringing it to the cabana in the mornings to share with other guests. It was a lovely gesture and greatly appreciated. When she returned to Canada, her departure left a void. Management immediately stepped into the breach and made an institution out of the morning coffee time.

The blowing of a conch shell at 10 a.m. daily signals that coffee, tea, and slices of fresh pineapple are ready for guests, and they are encouraged to take a rest from resting and enjoy each other's company. Attending the coffee time is a duty for the senior staff—Jack, Dorothy, the comptroller, restaurant manager, front office manager, executive housekeeper—and makes for a nice, happy relationship between guests and staff. One guest remarked that these parties were more fun than cocktail parties because a person could remember who they met and what they said! On rainy mornings, Irish coffee is served to keep "spirits" up!

The Millars chuckle when they recall one coffee party morning. Years ago, there was a woman visiting the resort who had fallen in love with Napili Kai. Perhaps it is true that when people fall in love with a vacation spot, they are blind to anything that might mar their pleasure.

This particular woman had been at Napili Kai for two weeks and had immersed herself in Napili Kai's atmosphere and all of the activities. One Wednesday morning, she had walked up from the beach to enjoy the 10 a.m. coffee party. She was in her bathing suit, and it was obvious that she was enjoying herself thoroughly. One of the staff, who knew her departure date, asked her how she thought she was going to get to her plane in time.

"Oh, I don't have to leave until Wednesday," she replied cheerily.

The staff member told her that this day was Wednesday. At first, she refused to believe him. Nor would she believe the people standing near her. When she was finally convinced, she broke into tears!

Preparations for a Lahaina Wing parking lot, 1963.

Certainly, when one is enjoying him or herself in a special haven, time means nothing: the surroundings and the people one meets mean everything!

Coffee time in the cabana is also a time when guests, if they have something on their minds, can complain directly to the senior staff. Once, when Jack was at the 10 a.m. party, he tensed when he saw a certain elderly couple coming in his direction.

Two days earlier, the woman had caused Jack's blood pressure to soar. Jack, Marg, and Dorothy had been sitting on the deck of the Teahouse enjoying a delightful lunch and watching the high surf. The 'no swimming' sign had been posted, and beach activity was restricted to sunbathing. Suddenly, cries for help caught their attention. An elderly man was on the sand, and he was waving to and hollering at a woman who was in the water and unable to return to shore.

Jack, sprang from his chair and rushed to the beach to be her savior! He grabbed the surfboard which was kept for rescue purposes, dropped his trousers on the sand— so as not to ruin his brand new pants—and, in his undershorts, madly paddled through the waves. She was just outside the reef.

When Jack reached her, she was somewhat hysterical and wouldn't listen to his instructions. Eventually, he got her on the surfboard. However, she kept rolling off into the water. Finally, Jack got her crosswise on the board. Jack, who was kicking furiously to push the surfboard, looked over his shoulder and saw a large wave rolling toward them.

He resigned himself to riding the wave toward shore. All was fine until the wave dumped Jack and his charge onto a patch of reef. The pounding bruised them, the sharp coral cut them, and both Jack and the elderly woman were quite upset by the time they made it back to the beach. By that time, people had gathered to help the bedraggled twosome.

Once she was safely on shore and the woman was no longer hysterical, Jack's concern gave way to anger.

"If I ever find you in that water again when that sign is posted, I'll kick your ass!" fumed Jack.

He stomped off to retrieve his trousers. Needless to say, all of this action had caused quite a scene for all the diners who were having lunch!

Well, when Jack saw this couple coming down the sidewalk toward him at the cabana coffee party two days later, he tensed. Expecting the man to threaten Jack with a suit for humiliating his wife, Jack was surprised by the man's cordiality. Imagine Jack's disbelief when the man, who had a camera in his hands, said,

"I'd like to have a photograph of the man who told my wife he'd kick her in the ass if she ever did that again. That's something I've never had the guts to do!"

They all laughed heartily and parted... and the couple returned for many years afterwards to Napili Kai.

Puna II, which opened in 1974, was run in the same manner as the Lani Wing. The Millars obtained the "Whitmar" property, situated between Puna Point and the Lani Wing, for the Puna II addition. Part of the agreement was that they would exhibit the family's prized rock collection in the stone wall of the downstairs lobby. The rocks were carefully chipped from their positions in the "Whitmar" fireplace and later placed in the lobby wall. A log is posted beside the wall which identifies the numbered rocks, telling where and how the stones were collected. A bronze plaque rests in the wall, dedicating the exhibit and describing the days of "Whitmar."

Another Whitmar legacy was a giant banyan which grew on the grounds. It had grown so that two large opposing limbs had crossed, forming an upside-down heart in the airspace between them. Jack decided that he wanted this tree—whose stump measured 30 inches in diameter—for the front of the building. He envisioned looking through the heart and seeing the front portico of the building: what a dramatic entrance!

Well, Napili Kai Beach Club had the tree trimmed to a height of ten feet by chain saws, keeping the larger limbs. Then, a trench was dug around its base, and the roots were cut. The trench was filled with fertilizer, and the tree was

The original furnishings for the Tea House about 1965.

allowed to rest for a year to recover from the surgery! Then, the tree was transported with a crane to a large pit, which had beem similarly prepared, at the new site. The tree was placed in the new trench with its roots covered with topsoil and bags of fertilizer and was kept moist. The tree survived and is now 36–40 inches across its base, growing exactly where Jack wanted it... almost. Somehow in the transplanting, the tree was turned so that the view through the heart is not as originally planned.

The Millars' philosophy has always been to enable a guest to have a wonderful stay at the resort. They encourage sociability in many other ways besides the coffee gatherings. For instance, if rain continues for a few days' duration, management invites all of the houseguests to attend a Rain-Ending Party in the Down Under Lounge, where guests are the hotel's guests and propose toasts to the end of the rain. Generally, the rain disappears before the party starts; but the party is held anyway and makes for hilarity!

The "cottage" viewed from across the putting green.

A Putting Party is held regularly on Monday nights. Foursomes are matched by the staff, and playing with one's spouse or roommate is prohibited. At 4:30 p.m. a shotgun start begins the party, and the twosome teams begin putting. At any time, if a player raises a putter, a cocktail waitress dashes to take an order. Since a drink costs only 50 cents for the occasion, a player can feel like a big shot and order for the foursome for the exhorbitant fee of $2—charged to his room.

The tournament lasts about an hour, and the winners are declared. Both the best score and the highest score are announced, and the bar flows freely. Then, a person—generally, a stockholder or a returned guest—is named to be the host for a round of drinks. The designee is usually stunned... but the bill is picked up by Napili Kai! Tuesday seems to be the friendliest day at the resort with so many people talking about the previous evening's fun.

When the hotel saw how successful the putting parties were, management decided to try another idea: why not have a cocktail party? Their intent was to have a slightly more formal occasion than the putting parties. Thus, the Wednesday evening Mai Tai party came into existence. The poolside parties have a receiving line of the senior staff and Jack and provide a wonderful opportunity for the guests to intermingle. Guests enjoy the camaraderie as well as the opportunity to show off their new muumuus and aloha shirts!

A great deal of social activity centers around the hotel's hot pool, christened the Hankipanki Pool by Jay Jacobus, a Napili Kai director. The demand for a hot pool was so great that in 1977 Napili Kai changed the small 20-foot diameter pool in front of the Aloha Wing into the largest hot pool in Hawaii.

The Hanki Panki Pool.

The pool, which has 12 jets, can be occupied by 20 people at once. Policy-setting was a challenge for management since it became such a popular area. The rules disallow children's use of the pool after noon and all use after 11 p.m.

Until it became a hot pool, the rooms overlooking it were not popular. Napili Kai management has been surprised that these rooms now are requested more than any other. Could it be that the Hankipanki Pool lives up to its name, offering a fringe benefit to guests as they sit on their balconies in the evenings and imagine?

Not all guests are as affectionate toward one another as those in the hotpool. Dorothy recalls a couple of fighting honeymooners! The irate husband proceeded to throw, missing his wife, the lanai furniture into the swimming pool. She retaliated and cut off the pant legs on all of his trousers!

Napili Kai, in its romantic setting, has been a honeymoon spot for many couples over the years. In 1964, a young honeymooning couple checked in with Ruth at the front desk. Ruth, who guessed they were about 16 years old and had run away from home, thought they were a darling couple and remarked repeatedly about them to Dorothy. Dottie was on the lookout for them but was unsuccessful in spotting them.

A week later, Dorothy asked Ruth about a good-looking young couple—with the young woman on crutches—whom Dorothy had observed walking around the property. Indeed, this was 'the darling couple.' Somehow, the bride had fallen between the twin beds in their room and had broken her leg!

Other couples have tried to hide their feelings. Late one evening after the staff and maids had gone home, two elderly couples checked in. Dot escorted one couple to a room and made sure they were comfortable, and then she went to see how Ruth's couple was doing.

"Oh, my! A king-size bed! I can't sleep with my husband; and, in fact, I won't! I haven't done so in years!" the woman was saying to Ruth.

Ruth and Dorothy assured the woman that a roll-away bed would be brought immediately. Well, since the staff had departed, Ruth and Dorothy had to carry the roll-away bed to the couple's room. The two women placed the bed alongside the king-size bed and were about to put on the sheets when the woman said,

"Oh, not so close!"

When Dorothy and Ruth left the room, Ruth jokingly said to the woman,

"Don't let me find out you haven't used it!"

Curiosity was too great for Ruth and Dottie to let the next day pass without checking with the maids. Upon inquiring, Dottie learned that the bed had not been used...nor was it ever used during the two weeks the couple stayed at Napili Kai! Who was fooling whom!

Despite the friendly atmosphere at Napili Kai, some guests are troublemakers. Such was the case with a woman many years ago. She complained to Dot that she had left her wristwatch in a specific location in her room and that when she had returned to her unit after a swim, her watch was missing. Her immediate claim was that one of the maids had stolen it. Dorothy was incensed to think that she thought that one of the staff would do such a thing. Well, the woman yelled and screamed, threatening to sue Napili Kai and demanding the police.

Of course, Dorothy immediately informed the house-keeping department. Later that day, one of the maids brought the wristwatch to Dottie. Dot summoned the guest to the front desk to identify the piece. The woman's response was that she had known that if she were loud enough, the watch would turn up. After she'd carried on in such a manner for a few minutes, Dorothy glared at her and asked her if she wanted to know where the watch had been found. Suddenly, the woman turned scarlet, grabbed her watch, and disappeared; and, Dorothy did not see her again although the woman stayed at Napili Kai for two more weeks! The watch had been found in the room next door to hers amongst the bedsheets by the head housekeeper and a maid. And...the room had been

Original Tea House of the Maui Moon, 1965.

occupied by a man who had been traveling alone!

Hotel-keeping is peppered with many light moments thanks to the assortment of guests. One elderly gentleman provided such a moment out of his concern for Napili Kai's establishment—a pleasant change from guests who have total disregard for property other than their own! After a swim in the ocean, this man was so concerned about taking sand into his room that he stepped out of his trunks outside his front door. It wasn't until he had trouble with his key in the lock that he realized he was at the wrong door!

As was mentioned earlier, the founders of Napili Kai Beach Club were all good friends, and this friendly circle expanded as other acquaintances were invited to join the corporation. Later, many guests who had returned annually over a long period of time became shareholders. The members of the corporation resisted bringing newcomers into the organization because the directors did not want to change the ways in which the resort functioned.

The directors sought to maintain the friendly, easy-going style that had characterized Napili Kai. To buy a share was to join the Napili Kai 'family': to belong to a club and be a part of the beautiful location. Today, the corporation numbers approximately 150 shareholders (all life members)—of about 70 different family units since many life members are sons, daughters, or spouses of other members.

The high point of the year for the life members is a week's stay at the time of the annual shareholders' meeting. In fact, the actual meeting is but a small part of the week-long festivities! Generally, 100 life members gather at Napili Kai for this gala.

An enormous tent is raised on one of the putting greens, and the tent is the formal headquarters for the many functions. Besides the almost-nightly round of cocktail parties and banquets, other activities are organized: golf, bridge, putting, tennis, cribbage, and shuffleboard tournaments! One life member, usually the prior year's winner, is the director for each event and individual trophies can be found in the lobby.

On the last night, which is always a Saturday, shareholders, hotel guests, and the department heads are invited to a dinner floor show and dancing. The merriment lasts long into the night!

The prize-giving, an event emceed by Dorothy, is done on Sunday under the big tent. Soups, beer, and wine are served, and a good time is had until guests leave for the airport.

This life members' week is a wonderful time for all of the them. Besides the meeting, the week provides a time for fellowship between people who have come from different parts of Canada and the United States. New ideas, as well as people, are introduced, and everyone is happy.

In 1980 Jack readied a surprise for the shareholders' pleasure at their annual meeting. 1980 was Napili Kai's 20th

Anniversary, and Jack wanted to mark this milestone year with something unusual. He sought to create a hallmark which would be visible both from the street and from the resort grounds. Finally, he settled on a form which he felt would be both unusual and distinctive and would be in keeping with the traditional Hawaiian use of lava.

Much discussion with the Maui Planning Commission ensued as they felt the structure was a sign and would be much too high and elaborate for the area. However, once they decided that the structure was a symbol, they became enthusiastic about it—although they placed a severe limitation on its height.

A trapezoidal lava pylon was erected, and a carved wood plaque was mounted near the top. Jack surrounded the monument with mature palm trees, planted grass, and named the area Napili's Anniversary Garden.

Shareholders and many guests gathered for the blessing by Reverend Charles Burger from the Church of the Holy Innocents in Lahaina and the dedication of this pylon. The entire monument was draped in a gigantic plumeria (frangipani) lei, which Jack cut to unveil the stones. Music filled the air, and speeches were given by many of the resort's original directors.

The main lobby, 1985.

CHAPTER TEN

Nightmare Revisited

Rain and its attendant flooding have not been the only disaster with which the Millars have had to contend over the years. A fire in 1984 caused a lot of damage to Napili Kai.

Jack, Marg, and Dorothy were spending a quiet evening at their "Gray Rocks" home when word of a fire at the hotel reached them. They attempted to phone the resort, but the switchboard was not functioning. So, Dorothy and Marg dashed to the hotel to assess the situation. Jack stayed home to telephone (all other phones being out) the maintainance personnel, senior department heads, and staff. His frustration mounted by the minute because it was a Saturday night and only a few of the people he sought to reach were home.

When Dorothy and Marg arrived at the hotel, firefighters were already on the scene—bashing with axes at the huge glass door. Dorothy screamed at the men to desist because she would let them in with her key, but they ignored her. Once they gained entry, the firefighters, outfitted with gas masks, smashed down the doors in the accounting office and sprayed water everywhere.

Apparently, the switchboard machinery in the basement had caught fire—most likely due to a short circuit. The basement area had filled with a dense black smoke, and the fire had spread to the basement ceiling. The front desk area was immediately above the fire, and the concrete floor became so hot that the lineoleum flooring buckled. The flames shot up through the switchboard conduit hole from the basement and got into the switchboard itself. Black smoke passed through the electrical conduits which led to the rooms in that building so that black smoke issued from the electrical outlets in those units.

Confusion was rife during the fire. A man from the electric company arrived while the fire was underway, climbed the utility pole opposite the building, and shut off all power leading to the hotel. Napili Kai Beach Club was plunged into total darkness, which added to the chaos.

The fire trucks exhausted their oxygen supply and had to send someone to Lahaina to buy more tanks from the dive shops. One fireman had a terrible time outfitting himself, trying to figure out what to don first: the gas mask or his protective clothing. He chose the former, only to find his protective jacket wouldn't fit over the mask. Next, he tried putting on the jacket first. But, then the cord which ran from the tank to the mask wouldn't fit in unless he tried to work it through a sleeve. Ten minutes later, he figured out that he needed to put on the jacket first, then the tank, and then the mask... and then connect the two!

Blinding smoke was everywhere, and an acrid stench filled the air. The latter became Napili Kai's greatest nightmare during the cleanup phase.

Never was the coconut wireless more effective than on the night of the fire! The Millars were touched that although the hotel phone system was dead, the entire management staff arrived at Napili Kai to render assistance. A communications network based on aloha had rapidly spread the news that Napili Kai was in trouble. Once the guests were evacuated from their rooms, the staff set up reservation charts in the Teahouse Restaurant and relocated everyone. Bill Wales and Dorothy accompanied the guests, once the firemen had granted permission, to their rooms so that they could collect their valuables and what they needed for one night and settled the guests in new rooms. Staff members volunteered to stay throughout the night to insure that no one pilfered the rooms.

The fire left Napili Kai in a terrible state of confusion because the basement was truly the heart of the hotel operation. The basement housed the laundry, housekeeping, accounting, files, and records. So many records were destroyed in the fire. Luckily, the reservations records were not amongst them for if they had been, future bookings for a year or more of scheduled guests would have been lost, and Napili Kai would have had no idea of who was coming or when!

Another lucky thing was that the inventories were not damaged beyond reading so that Napili Kai was able to prove the value of the loss to the insurance company and be recompensed.

Restoration after the fire was a ghastly task. Getting rid of the stench seemed an impossibility. Staying in the rooms, even with open doors, was barely tolerable. The smell had ruined the mattresses, pillows, bedding, and curtains; so although the flames had not burned furnishings, the smell rendered them useless, and they had to be disgarded.

Crews attacked the restoration project. They started by shoveling out the basement and hauling truckloads of material to the dump. Then, the basement walls, floor, and ceiling were scrubbed with a special chemical which was supposed to impart a sweeter smell to the area! Jack had been cautioned against attempting to paint out the smell. He had been told that the smell would come through the paint!

Many of the office walls were plasterboard and consequently had been damaged by the water. So, many walls needed to be rebuilt. Rebuilding the laundry was the highest priority, and while that monumental challenge was underway, Napili Kai borrowed sheets and sent the linen to a commercial laundry.

Four months elapsed while Napili Kai struggled in the aftermath of the fire. Napili Kai raced to get ready for full occupancy in that building again before the annual shareholders' meeting on the second Wednesday of November. Imagine how relieved everyone was when the deadline was met and operations returned to normal!

CHAPTER ELEVEN

Living The Dream

Looking backwards in time, certain changes on Maui stand out prominently. Until 1970, accommodating tourists fell primarily to the few resorts in Kaanapali, Hana, and Kahului. Then, the condominum explosion occurred, and Maui's complex on changed considerably.

Developers and builders streamed to Maui and bought or leased land parcels which they developed to maximum density. High-rise monstrosities, some looking more like jails than resorts, speckled the shoreline. Little thought was given to the creation of an atmosphere wherein people could enjoy themselves the way they do elsewhere in resorts which have been built by shareholders or corporations who strive to provide an attractive holiday experience for guests. Many of the condominums were little more than stacks of corridors and rooms, surrounded by parking lots.

There was a rash of unbelievable prices, and many unsuspecting mainland people purchased units because they thought their investment would explode in value. The builders quickly disappeared from the scene, and the motive behind expansion seemed only to be to sell at a profit.

This mood and its resultant face saddened Jack Millar whose dream has always been to enrich a person's life with a beautiful, tropical experience. Jack worked hard to preserve the ambiance which is such a special part of the Napili Kai Beach Club. He wanted to protect the large investment that the corporation had put into their lovely, low-rise resort so Jack approached Robert Ohata, the newly appointed planning director. Ohata suggested that Jack petition the County Council to form a separate zone for Napili Bay which would later be known as the Napili Bay Civic Improvement District and write in the restrictions which would preserve its desireable state.

Jack canvassed Napili, speaking to the landowners. They were delighted to incorporate their properties into this zone where certain restrictions would exist: no building could be higher than a tree, an architectural committee would be appointed to oversee color harmony, buildings would be in a Hawaiian style, the only function permitted other than residential would be that of a resort-hotel, and that no more than 25% of a piece of property could be built upon in order to minimize density.

An attorney drew up the document which was passed to the Council for its inspection. Happily, this zoning bylaw was passed on May 16, 1964. At that time, no one envisioned the extent of the building yet to come.

Later, people began to realize how valuable their land had become were it available for high-rise development. Jack suspects he did not make any friends during this period in Napili Kai's history; but, today, it is delightful to see Napili Kai's low-rise profile. Certainly, it is a pleasure for all of the guests who visit Napili Bay.

Napili Kai felt the consequence of the burgeoning condominium sales in that a large number of guests who would return annually to the resort bought units and no longer had a need for the hotel. They, in turn, rented their units to other former Napili Kai guests; so, Napili Kai Beach Club's incidence of returning guests declined markedly.

Today, 206 separate condominium resorts operate in daily transient rentals as compared to only 11 corporate resorts, including the Wailea hotels and the Hyatt. The competition from the condominums makes the corporate operations difficult in that the latter must pay half of its profits to the government by way of a corporate tax. A condominium owner, on the other hand, can charge off his or her individual losses against other income. Thus, the government becomes the major competitor to the corporate resort, which must work to the bottom line in order to pay the mortgage, the staff, and still produce a profit for shareholders.

The bubble has burst for many of the individuals who tried to buy paradise at Maui's expense. A large number of condominiums are now held by the banks because the buyer failed to make the payments. Many of these units cannot be sold for the amount of the mortgages; so, the banks, hoping for some appreciation, hold the condominiums.

The condominium explosion of the '70s had yet another effect on Maui. Maui does not have an adequate government infrastructure for handling the expanded population. Island roads, schools, staff housing, police coverage, and hospital care are not sufficient to meet the population's needs.

1985, Napili Kai's 25th Anniversary year, has been an exciting time. The Teahouse of the Maui Moon was re-modeled and renamed the Sea House Restaurant. White lattice, hanging fern baskets, and a new menu gave the dining room a delightfully new look.

One of 1985's most satisfying events has been the start of the dam-building project, a project which was finally approved by the Congress, Senate, and the President. The first of the holding basins has already been installed in the south end of Napili Bay and protects that section from further flooding and muddy runoff. The north end project, valued at $2.7 million, which will protect the north end of Napili Bay is scheduled to start in November, 1985. The advent of this flood-protection system is a great moment for Napili Kai Beach Club because it eliminates forever the threat of future flooding damage to the properties in the lower area. Because the underground pipe will empty into the ocean as far out as the reef line and the shore current carries the water from the rocky north shore out to sea, the muddy water from heavy rains will not affect the clean water in the bay.

Another exciting prospect is the acquisition of the leased land under the Lahaina Wing. The corporation now has an option to buy this land before the end of the year and intends to exercise that option. By purchasing that property, the corporation will consolidate the land into a block, devoid of individual property lines. Coupled with the fact that the dam

will protect the land from flooding, the opportunity to purchase this property looks extremely exciting!

Once this property has been bought, Napili Kai plans to add 44 units to the resort, developing it as an overall new complex. An architect has been selected and has produced some preliminary designs and drawings which convey what the new cottages will look like. Essentially, the cottages will have high, Hawaiian roofs. Each of the two-story cottages

will have three rooms on each floor which will interconnect as suites or rent independently. The cottages will be strategically positioned around the large putting greens so that guests can enjoy a green expanse as well as a magnificent view of the ocean.

When expansion money has been needed in the past, Jack has traditionally gone to individuals before institutions; and, for that reason, a new share issue is currently being circulated to shareholders and return guests in order to raise a minimum of $1 million. There is no question that the property will be purchased by Napili Kai; but, as always, the resort wants to give the shareholders and guests—new guests as well—a chance to participate in this exciting development.

The Millars attribute Napili Kai's special ambiance to the friendships and personal involvement which has characteristically sprung up amongst Napili Kai members.

Jack's enthusiasm and excitement for this new share offering is clear. For him, additional new shareholders mean a widening of the Napili Kai family.

After the development of the lower beach lands, which will add nicely to the resort's profit, the corporation has no desire for further expansion. It does not wish to acquire any more land; nor, does the board intend to buy additional buildings.

Rather, the corporation wishes to devote all of its energy to improving existing conditions, to maintain the club-like atmosphere which is such an enjoyable feature of the resort, to encourage the continuance of the friendliness which abounds, and to keep the resort's Hawaiian feeling. In short, the Napili Kai Beach Club and its full corporate organization has become the dreamer, reaching out to provide happiness for all who enter Napili Kai's doors.

Past and present directors whose unstinting gift of their time guided Napili Kai:

R. C. 'Cece' Atkinson	Vancouver, B.C.
W. T. G. 'Bill' Atwood	Vancouver, B.C.
H. E. 'Herb' Bliss	Vancouver, B.C.
A. T. R. 'Tommy' Campbell	Vancouver, B.C.
A. 'Alex' Campbell	Vancouver, B.C.
L. S. 'Chip' Chipperfield	New Westminster, B.C.
M. J. 'Del' de La Mothe	Vancouver, B.C.
R. R. 'Dick' Heppe	Los Angeles, Cal.
J. M. 'Jay' Jacobus	San Francisco, Cal.
R. M. 'Don' Johnston	Vancouver, B.C.
G. M. 'Gerald' Knowlton	Calgary, Alt.
L. M. 'Les' Little	Vancouver, B.C.
Dr. E. C. 'Tim' McCoy	Vancouver, B.C.
D. 'Dot' Millar	Maui, HI
J. C. 'Jack' Millar	Maui, HI
J. D. 'Dewey' Millar	Honolulu, HI
M. R. 'Margaret' Millar	Maui, HI
S. C. 'Steve' Saunders	Everett, Wash.
W. A. 'Bill' Speers	Vancouver, B.C.
V. 'Vic' Thorson	Vancouver, B.C.
J. V. 'Jim' Wall	San Francisco, Cal.
E. S. 'El' Williams	San Francisco, Cal.
W. A. 'Bill' Wilson	Los Angeles, Cal.

A Flood of Support

The November 13th, 1985, annual meeting of Napili Kai shareholders became the focal point of several different and secretive plans. This was the resort's silver anniversary, 25 years of struggle and success. Management planned a great celebration and a number of shareholders made plans of their own.

To augment the celebration, management put together two very special gifts. Artist Joyce Clark, of Hana, was commissioned to paint Napili Bay depicting the area and the resort. Many canvas-backed prints were made and a copy distributed to each shareholder. This book, *The Unbeatable Dream*, was the second gift. It was clandestinely produced in a ninety day crash program with copies delivered to the shareholders two days before the meeting.

The 25th annual meeting was jammed by 203 participants bringing fellowship and joy to the renewal of acquaintances and the silver celebration. They also brought a couple of surprises of their own. The Board of Directors, spurred by Vice President Dick Heppe and his lovely wife, Patricia, developed the notion of giving a scholarship in Jack's name as a special presentation during the meeting. The presentation took the form of a large unframed sheet of paper on which was embossed a cheque made out to "Jack Millar Scholarship Fund" in the amount of $3,000 and signed by virtually all of the shareholders in attendance. As a surprised and ecstatic Jack Millar received the presentation, one of the shareholders, Gerald McQuarrie, doubled the size of the fund.

Management in the person of Jack Millar declared that the scholarship monies would be used for the higher education of the graduates of the Napili Kai Foundation and also for the higher education of any special member of the staff's families. Further, he stated that his family, Margaret, Dorothy, Dewey and Elizabeth, would be directors and that the fund would be a non-profit entity soliciting contributions for its development. Jack was more thrilled by this voluntary gesture of esteem for him than anything he could remember in his long and eventful life. He retired that evening with his scholarship in hand to "think nice thoughts about its future." In the first few days thereafter enough donations were received to make it obvious that some deserving student would be awarded aid in 1986.

The Jack Millar Scholarship Fund, however, was not the end of the shareholders' and guests' business with Jack. In the last chapter of this book the project to purchase and develop the half-acre of land under the Lahaina Wing was put forward. Such an action would complete the purchase of Napili Kai lands and see the last graceful expansion of resort facilities. The proposed money-raising share issue caught the imagination and sympathies of shareholders and guests alike. Subscription took off like a rocket, and by the time the annual meeting was brought to a close, sufficient new funds had been subscribed to more than purchase the land. And so the option to buy the last half-acre was exercised and the land duly registered in Napili Kai's name.

To cap this marvelous achievement and flood of spontaneous support a traditional Hawaiian ceremony was held on December 17, 1985, to bless the land. Father Keahi of Lahaina's Maria Lanakila Church presided with the Millar family, friends, guests and staff in attendance.

Jack, Dorothy and Margaret Millar with Father Keahi at the blessing.

Meanwhile the share issue continued to grow, and the million dollar goal was subscribed by December 31st, 1985. With this last major hurdle overcome the persistent dream of twenty-five years matures.